Pondering, Praying, Preaching

Romans 8

Bonnie Thurston

SLG Press
Convent of the Incarnation
Fairacres Parker Street
Oxford OX4 1TB England
www.slgpress.co.uk

ISBN: 978-0-7283-0300-3

ISSN: 0307-1405

Cover Image: Icon of St Paul the apostle, written by a Nun of New Skete.

*In thanksgiving for the hospitality, sustenance and friendship of
the Sisters of the Love of God, Oxford
and for shared ministry with Chapel Hill Christian Church
Brooke County, West Virginia, USA.*

CONTENTS

INTRODUCTION

Professor Luke Timothy Johnson speaks for many New Testament scholars when he writes that Paul's letter to the Romans is 'considered the central writing of the Pauline corpus for its subject matter as well as its length, power, and clarity of argument.'[1] Romans is Paul's theological magnum opus. N. T. Wright notes that although Romans 'is neither systematic theology nor a summary of Paul's life work ... it is by common consent his masterpiece. It dwarfs most of his other writings.'[2] J. D. G. Dunn describes it as the Apostle's 'most important' letter 'being the first well-developed theological statement by a Christian theologian which has come down to us, and which has had incalculable influence on the framing of Christian theology ever since — arguably the single most important work of Christian theology ever written.'[3] It is certainly one which has shaped Christian theology and practice — for good and ill.

St Augustine, perhaps the most influential theologian in the Western church, was steeped in the thought of Romans. Martin Luther, the Augustinian monk of Wittenberg, prepared lectures on Romans which subsequently changed the face of the church and the map of Europe. John Calvin created a Protestant systematic theology based, according to some theological historians, on Romans 8. John Wesley's Methodist revival resulted from his hearing Luther's 'Preface to Romans' read at a

---

[1] Luke Timothy Johnson, *The Writings of the New Testament*, Revised Edition (Minneapolis: Fortress Press, 1999), 343.
[2] N. T. Wright, 'The Letter to the Romans,' in *The New Interpreters Bible* Vol. 10, Leander E. Keck, Senior New Testament Editor (Nashville: Abingdon, 2002), 10: 395. Hereafter in text as NIB.
[3] J. D. G. Dunn, 'Romans, Letter to the' in *Dictionary of Paul and His Letters*, G. Hawthorne, R. Martin, D. Reid, eds. (Downers Grove, IL & Leicester: InterVarsity Press, 1993), 838. Hereafter in text and notes as DPL.

Moravian meeting. Karl Barth used his commentary on Romans to set forth a version of Christianity now referred to as 'neo-orthodoxy.'[4] N. T. Wright reminds us that this 'catalogue could be balanced by a similar number who have radically mis-understood [Romans]. Troublingly, the lists would overlap.' (NIB 10:395)

In light of all this, perhaps Romans should be considered a dangerous letter. Certainly it sets forth major theological ideas of Christianity: sin, grace, justification, redemption, election, repentance, love. Romans is Paul's most complete and mature expression of the doctrine of justification. It is not, however, a summary of Pauline thought as it does not treat, for example, the Lord's Supper/Last Supper/Eucharist, resurrection, or the *parousia* (return or second coming of Jesus Christ), although it alludes to it. It is not a complete statement of a Pauline system, if indeed he had one. Nevertheless, the centrality of Romans is not in dispute. It is usually studied in the context of Paul's thought, even as Paul is usually studied as a New Testament theologian, and often as a pugilistic and quarrelsome one. But suppose one approached this important letter from another direction or understood Paul himself differently? How might this affect how Romans is read and interpreted?

Rowan Williams' sparkling and incisive small book, *Meeting God in Paul*, which I highly recommend as an introduction to Paul, begins with the observation that people 'are quite likely to have picked up a set of assumptions about Paul' and that 'these

---

[4] For concise historical summaries of the work's interpretation see Brendan Byrne, SJ, 'Interpreting Romans: The New Perspective and Beyond,' *Interpretation* 58/3 (July, 2004), 241–252; John D. Godsey, 'The Interpretation of Romans in the History of The Christian Faith,' *Interpretation* 34/1 (Jan. 1980), 3–16; Robert Jewett, 'Major Impulses in the Theological Interpretation of Romans Since Barth,' *Interpretation* 34/1 (Jan. 1980), 17–31; and Albert Schweitzer, *Paul and His Interpreters* (New York: Macmillan, 1951).

half-understood assumptions obscure nearly everything of what makes Paul really interesting and exciting.'[5] I could not agree more, and have for some years been working toward a book-length study focusing on Paul as a man of prayer, what we might call a 'spiritual director'. It is in this context, and that of regular preaching on readings from the lectionary, that I became intrigued by Romans 8 in this, Paul's 'central', letter.

Like Christian theologians, the church's liturgists have taken Romans very seriously as well. In the common lectionary used by Roman Catholics, Anglicans, and most 'main-line' Protestants, in year A on at least twelve Sundays in Ordinary Time, a text from Romans is the epistle appointed for the primary service. Four of these are from Romans 8, as is the epistle for Trinity Sunday in some years. Thomas G. Long, in his article, 'Preaching Romans Today', also notes the prominence given to Romans in the lectionary. 'Around two dozen selections from Romans appear in the most frequently used lectionaries, and the calendar in year A affords the poss-ibility of some modest *lectio continua* preaching through the central chapters of the epistle.'[6]

Additionally, Romans 8 is the spacial centre of the letter; it summarizes the seven substantive chapters that precede it, and without denigrating the contents of Chapter 16, about the textual history of which there is significant scholarly discussion, seven chapters follow Chapter 8. In addition to being the 'hinge' chapter in the letter, Romans 8 summarizes the opening argument and prepares for the closing material. Romans 8 contains the heart of Paul's message in this letter and some of

---

[5] Rowan Williams, *Meeting God in Paul* (London: SPCK, 2015), ix–x.

[6] Thomas G. Long, 'Preaching Romans Today,' *Interpretation* 58/3 (July 2004), 266.

his most important spiritual teaching, as well as a summary of his thought about the Holy Spirit. I thought an accessible series of reflections on the chapter might be of value to those who will preach it, hear it repeatedly as part of the Sunday liturgy, and pray through its contents. I hope the following brief study will meet those goals, and I am very grateful to SLG Press for making it possible and available, especially to the editor, Sister Christine, and her assistant, Pinky Severn.

By and large, these meditations leave theology to the systematic theologians. They do not address, except perhaps tangentially, the major theme of Romans: God's righteousness. Wright suggests that '… Romans makes God and God's justice, love, and reliability its major themes.' (NIB 10: 403, note 11) Our study is not a series of exegetical notes, although it provides some in the 'Points of Interest' sections, but a product of exegetical work. Nor does it tell the reader how to pray or what to preach, although I hope the reflections and the material in the 'For Prayer and Pondering' sections will stimulate both. It probably goes without saying that creative preaching and praying with any given scriptural passages occur within the parameters of the text and its times. That being the case, I have provided a brief introduction to aspects of Paul's letter to the Romans that might bear on our understanding of Romans 8. Perhaps akin to the evil spirits in Mark 5, the critical literature on Romans is legion. By means of footnotes, I have provided links to some classical studies and critical scholarly issues should a reader want to pursue them. You may wish to skip the background and thematic outline material, but I hope you will not.

Finally, I have been engaged with Romans as a university and seminary professor, a preacher, and a pray-er of the Daily Office for many years. While I have striven properly to document the ideas of others, to give credit where credit is due, I may have overlooked something or someone. Any omission is entirely unintended, and I would be grateful to have it pointed out so that correction could be made in any future editions of this very mere study. Of course, N. T. Wright's quip in his 'Letter to the Romans' in *The New Interpreter's Bible* is entirely correct, '… anyone who claims to understand Romans fully is, almost by definition, mistaken' (NIB 10: 395). I make no such claim.

For I am not ashamed of the Gospel; it is the power of God for salvation to everyone who has faith, to the Jew first and also to the Greek. For in it the righteousness of God is revealed through faith for faith; as it is written, 'The one who is righteous will live by faith.' **(Rom. 1:16–17)**

BACKGROUND:
HISTORICAL & LITERARY

The City of Rome[7]

At the time of Paul's epistle, Rome was the most important city in the Roman Empire, the greatest city in the West. In the eighth century BC Etruscans from the northwest overran and settled the area. In 500 BC the Romans threw off Etruscan rule and established the Roman Republic which lasted until the formation of the First Triumvirate in 60 BC. From that group, Julius Caesar emerged in 48 BC as acknowledged master of Rome. His rule laid the foundation for the Roman Empire and the *Pax Romana* under which the Empire flourished and which, perhaps paradoxically, assisted the spread of Christianity.

As the hub for roads and communication, Rome was mistress of the Mediterranean. It had a diverse population of roughly a million from every known race of people. Rome boasted 28 libraries, 7 bridges, 8 large parks, 11 forums, 10 basilicas, 11 public baths, 19 aqueducts, and 29 principal roads. The Circus Maximus for chariot races held 50,000 as did the Coliseum.

Of the population of Rome, some 40,000 to 50,000 were Jews. Jewish presence in Rome is first recorded in 139 BC. Many more Jews were brought to Rome as slaves after Pompey conquered Jerusalem in 63 BC. Shortly thereafter, a delegation came from Roman Palestine to petition for better treatment of Jews. In the reign of Claudius (AD 41–45) all Jews were banished from Rome because of rioting over one 'Chrestus' (see Acts 18:2). When Nero became Emperor in AD 54, Jews were

---

[7] Mark Reasoner, 'Rome and Roman Christianity' in DPL, 850–855 provides a summary.

allowed to return and were given special privileges, including being allowed places of worship (there were 12 synagogues in the city), exemption from military service, and the ability to collect Temple taxes for Jerusalem. This did not endear them to the general population.[8] Dunn notes '… the Jewish community was both influential in Rome and deeply despised, not to say hated, by the most influential voices of the Roman intelligentsia' (DPL 839). All this, of course, coloured the Roman view of Christianity, as well. There were close political bonds between Rome and her client kingdoms, and this was true for Roman Palestine. Herodian princes, for example, were sent to Rome to be raised and educated. The Emperor Titus brought the Jewish King Agrippa II to Rome, and his sister, Berenice, apparently became Titus' mistress.

The religious pluralism of the Empire was evident in the city of Rome, but Roman religion itself was closely related to Roman government. For example, its priests advised the Senate, largely by augury. On the Capitolium, a temple dedicated to Jupiter, Juno, and Minerva dominated the city. Both in public and at home the performance of religious ritual was ubiquitous. The religious exclusivism of Judaism and Christianity was foreign to Roman religious practice.[9] Williams notes in *Meeting God in Paul* '… in this context nobody belongs to a "religion." There is no such thing as "*a* religion" in the first Christian

---

[8] The classic study on the Jews in Rome is H. J. Leon, *The Jews of Ancient Rome* (Philadelphia: Jewish Publication Society of America, 1960).

[9] A short, accessible introduction to the religious environment of Rome and early Christianity is Luther H. Martin, *Hellenistic Religions* (New York/Oxford: Oxford University Press, 1987). For more detailed treatment see C. Kerenyi, *The Religion of the Greeks and Romans* (London: Thames and Hudson, 1962); Han-Josef Klauck, *The Religious Context of Early Christianity* (Edinburgh: T & T Clark, 2000) and Helmut Koester, *Introduction to the New Testament*, Vol. 1 (Philadelphia: Fortress, 1982), especially section 6 'The Roman Empire as the Heir of Hellenism.'

7

century. People do religious things. … Being religious was part of being a citizen.'[10]

The Founding and Character of the Roman Church

The Roman church must have existed before AD 48/49 when Claudius expelled the Jews. Suetonius' report of the expulsion ordered by Claudius is the first written suggestion of a church in Rome, but that reference is inferential. Christianity was probably brought to Rome by Jewish Christians from Palestine. According to Acts 2:10 there were Romans, both Jews and proselytes, in attendance at Pentecost. Acts 18:2 suggests Paul's associates in Corinth, Priscilla and Aquila, were among those expelled. 'Church', of course, did not mean a building, but believers in Jesus as the Christ who met in a number of private homes in the city. The church reached Rome early in the apostolic era. Pseudo-Clement preserves a tradition of Barnabas preaching at Rome, and a widely-held theory places Peter there as early as AD 42. Christianity probably reached Rome before AD 50 and took its first followers from the synagogues. Paul's letter to Roman Christians is perhaps the earliest indisputable reference to Christianity there.

What characterized the church at Rome? Certainly there were both Jewish and Gentile believers. Matthew Black notes that '… the Roman church was of Jewish origin but of Gentile growth, and possibly, of predominantly Gentile racial composition. It was … a mixed community, socially as well as racially.'[11] One finds in the Roman letter evidence of the Jewish character of the church in Paul's on-going concern with Torah, his allusions to Hebrew scripture, and his use of the language

---

[10] Williams 22, 23.

[11] Matthew Black, *Romans*, NCBC 2nd edn (Grand Rapids: Eerdmans & London: Marshall, Morgan, & Scott, 1973), 5.

8

of Jewish worship. Of course, a major issue in the letter, and in early Christianity generally, is the relationship between Jews and Gentiles. One reason for the letter was to improve relations between those groups (e.g., the exhortation in 14:1–15:13).

What would it mean to say that Roman Christianity had a Jewish cast? It could mean Jewish Christians insisted on full observance of Torah. It could mean the church accepted the compromise solution that was reported in Acts 15. It could mean the Jewish Christians demanded no Jewish observances of Gentile converts, as Paul did not. It certainly meant the Roman church had strong ties to Jerusalem from whence many Roman Jews originally came. Mark Reasoner notes that '… Jewish Christianity retained a close connection with its Jewish roots in Jerusalem. Paul's letter to the church is evidence for this (Rom. 1:16; 3:1–30; 9–11), (DPL 853). If Peter were earlier resident in Rome, that would be another tie to the Jerusalem church.

The Reasons for the Letter

An important feature of the Roman letter is that Paul is writing to a community he has not visited. In this Romans is like Colossians. He prays that 'by God's will I may somehow at last succeed in coming to you' (1:10). This fact helps to explain why there are few references to concrete situations or personal news. Thus the tone of Romans is more formal, its style closer to Jewish apologetics, and Paul uses material not found elsewhere. Paul's circumstances are made clear in chapters 1 and 15. He is apparently in Corinth (Rom. 15:25–27; 2 Cor. 16:3–5; Acts 20–23) *c.*57/58, from whence he commends to the Roman church Phoebe, 'a deacon of the church at Cenchreae, so that you may welcome her in the Lord … she has been a benefactor of many and of myself as well' (16:1–2). Cenchreae is the port of Corinth, so Paul apparently entrusted this letter to her to deliver to Rome. Those who consider Paul a misogynist, might consider the full implications of this.[12] According to Acts 28:14–16, Paul arrived in Rome *c*.60 to stand trial before Nero's Praetorian Prefect. But that is *after* he wrote the letter.

Why did he write? There are a variety of plausible answers. Two classic reasons have been suggested. First, scholars suggest that in Romans Paul was occupied with his own concerns. He is writing both a summary of his theological and practical positions on issues, a sort of 'last will and testament', and hoping to solicit funds for a mission to Spain. Second, Paul is occupied with concerns of the Roman church. He wrote to address the Jew/Gentile issue there. Certainly, other historical reasons may have motivated the letter.

Paul is facing a trip to Jerusalem which he has reason to fear on two accounts. First, he will surely face cross-examination, if not persecution, from the Jewish authorities he has deserted. Second, he has reason to be uneasy that the Jerusalem church may not accept the collection he is bringing. For Paul, the motivation for that collection of funds from the relatively more prosperous Gentile churches for the impoverished Jerusalem church is to help strengthen the bonds between the growing Gentile church and the mother church at Jerusalem. The Roman letter may represent Paul's thinking as he faces problems connected with this situation.

Or, as 2 Corinthians 10–13 and the letter to the Galatians reveal, the churches in the northeast Mediterranean were rife with divisions and strife which spilled over into rebellion

---

[12] For more on Phoebe and Romans 16 see Bonnie Thurston 'Women in the New Testament: The Example of Romans 16,' in Edward J. Mahoney (ed.), *Scripture as the Soul of Theology* (Collegeville: Liturgical Press, 2005), 40–59.

against Paul's authority. In hopes of leaving all this behind, Paul wants to go to what is now Spain, which is unevangelized. Perhaps he wants to go where no one has preached Christ in order to avoid the problems and controversies over 'who's in charge'. Paul needs financial support for this mission, so he writes to establish contact with the growing and influential Roman church in hopes of getting it (see Rom. 15:22–33). He assures the Romans he will only pass through (15:24). Might the Roman church of Jewish origin have been uneasy about the repercussions of a visit by so difficult and controversial a figure?

We might summarize the major reasons for Paul's letter to the Romans as follows:

1. He wrote to summarize his thought because he knew his mission (and perhaps his life) was near its end.

2. He sought support for a mission to Spain (15:24, 28).

3. He was smarting from rebukes in Corinth and Galatia and wrote to defend himself and his ideas. That Paul employs the diatribe style (see p. 13–14 below) may suggest he thought the Gospel was under attack.

4. He wrote to help mediate tensions between Jewish and Gentile Christians (Rom. 9–11, 13; 14:1–15).

5. Barth, following Luther, maintained that a proper understanding of the Old Testament was one of Paul's major reasons for writing to Rome — perhaps an important point in view of Marcion's later use of Paul.[13]

---

[13] For more on the letter's origin see R. J. Karris, 'Rom. 14:1–15:13 and the Occasion of Romans', *Catholic Biblical Quarterly* 25 (1973), 155–178 and A. J. M. Wedderburn, *The Reason for Romans* (Edinburgh: T & T Clark, 1989).

Textual and Stylistic Considerations[14]

The authenticity of Romans has never been seriously questioned because to do so would involve questioning authorship of most of the Pauline letters. Romans is attested in both New Testament and Patristic writings. It is apparently quoted in 1 Peter, James, and Hebrews, and amongst the Apostolic Fathers by Clement of Rome, Ignatius of Antioch, and Polycarp. By AD 160 it was included in Marcion's Canon. There are interesting textual questions,[15] largely focused on chapter 16, but they are unrelated to chapter 8 and to our concerns in this brief monograph.

Paul's letter to the Romans follows the conventions of the Greco-Roman letter: an introductory formula, here unusually long, and thanksgiving; the body of and reason for the letter which, characteristically for Paul, closes with *parenesis*, practical instruction; and a conclusion formula, again extended in this letter.[16] In style, Romans might be called 'epistolary catechesis,' a letter written to instruct its recipients. While the diction and rhetoric is formal, it is also energetic. Considering the demographic make-up of the Roman church, it is not surprising that Romans reflects a distinctly Jewish literary character. It makes extensive use of scriptural quotation, including composite

---

[14] A summary is found in Dunn's entry on Romans in DPL, especially Section 4 'Literary Form and Coherence' (841–842). Major commentaries on Romans treat the matter extensively; and see Stanley K. Stowers, *Letter Writing in Greco-Roman Antiquity* (Philadelphia: Westminster Press, 1986).

[15] See Harry Gamble, Jr, *The Textual History of the Letter to the Romans* (Grand Rapids: Eerdmans, 1977).

[16] For more on the Greco-Roman letter see Jerome Murphy-O'Connor, *Paul the Letter-Writer* (Collegeville: Liturgical Press, 1995); Stanley K. Stowers, *Letter Writing in Greco-Roman Antiquity* (Philadelphia: Westminster, 1986); Jeffrey A. D. Weima, *Paul the Ancient Letter Writer* (Grand Rapids: Baker Academic, 2016).

quotations, and adaptations and interpretation some have likened to that at Qumran. Rabbinical methods of argumentation and argument by analogy are also in evidence.[17]

Perhaps the aspect of Paul's rhetoric in Romans that has received the most scholarly attention is his use of diatribe. Diatribe is a rhetorical form that originated in Hellenistic philosophical schools and, in the New Testament period, was prominent among the Stoics. There was a Stoic school in Tarsus which might account for the influence of Stoicism in Paul's writings. The diatribe form sets up a dialogue in which imaginary opponents, hypothetical scenarios, and false conclusions are introduced by the speaker or writer in order to clarify his own, correct, position, avoid misunderstandings, and forward the topic under discussion. The point of diatribe is not polemical, but to instruct and exhort. This is clearly exemplified in Paul's widespread use of vice and virtue lists, another Stoic pedagogical device.

Pauline diatribe is most evident in Romans, especially chapters 1–11 in which Paul addresses an imaginary interlocutor. It is also evident in the use of apostrophe and hyperbole, as well as in objections raised by the formulae 'What shall we say?' or 'What then?' and by rejections of the interlocutor's points with 'By no means!' — the famous *me genoito* — or 'Heaven forbid!' Luke Timothy Johnson notes 'The diatribe is not a formless rant but a structured form of

---

[17] Classic works on the subject include Joseph Bonsirven, SJ, *Exegese Rabbinique et Exegese Paulinienne* (Paris: Beauchesne: 1938/39); W. D. Davies, *Paul and Rabbinic Judaism* (London: SPCK, 1955); E. Earl Ellis, *Paul's Use of the Old Testament* (Edinburgh: Oliver and Boyd, 1957); E. P. Sanders, *Paul and Palestinian Judaism* (Philadelphia: Fortress/ London: SCM, 1977). In 'Paul the Jew' in *Meeting God in Paul*, Rowan Williams takes a very interesting point of view about Paul's Jewish lineage and the teaching tradition he inherited. See pp. 11–17.

argument.' He suggests the following features in this form of argument: 1. Thesis statement; 2. Demonstration by means of antithesis; 3. Thesis restated; 4. Demonstration of the thesis by example; 5. Further exposition of the thesis; 6) Answering objections to the thesis.[18] In his discussion of diatribe D. F. Watson correctly observes 'the use of diatribe in Romans does not indicate that Paul is engaging in polemic against Judaism ... or specific groups within the Roman congregation, but teaching the Romans his Gospel prior to his visit'.[19]

A Note on Interpretation of Romans

Largely as a result of studies of Paul and Judaism, we are in what some scholars call an interpretive era of a 'new perspective' on Paul.[20] Many trace it to Krister Stendahl's 1961 lecture to the American Psychological Association, 'The Apostle Paul and the Introspective Conscience of the West', which was published in his *Paul among Jews and Gentiles.*[21] Stendahl, a Swedish Lutheran, argued that Paul has been wrongly interpreted through the lens of the 'introspective conscience' which reads back onto Paul concerns that were not his. Eventually, 'Paul's whole theology, especially his idea of justification in Christ, gets strained through Luther's *Angst.'*[22] The Pauline corpus should not be read in the light of Romans 7:24–25 with a modern concern about guilt and unworthiness, or of Luther's psychology. On the contrary, Paul was more

---

[18] Johnson 346.

[19] D. F. Watson, 'Diatribe' in DPL 214; Stanley K. Stowers, *The Diatribe and Paul's Letter to the Romans*, SBLDS 57 (Chico, CA: Scholars, 1981).

[20] See J. D. G. Dunn, 'The New Perspective on Paul,' *Bulletin of the John Rylands Library* 65 (1983) 95–112. And see the list of primary themes in Byrne, 245–247.

[21] Krister Stendahl, *Paul Among Jews and Gentiles* (Philadelphia: Fortress, 1976).

[22] Long 267.

concerned about the relationship between Jews and Gentiles in the church.

Romans is about much more than an anguished individual. In *Final Account: Paul's Letter to the Romans*, Stendahl makes the case that Paul was concerned about two shameful theological problems: first, his own health, that 'thorn in the flesh' (2 Cor. 12:7) that God would not remove, and, second, that Israel was not accepting the Gospel.[23] 'The central question in Romans is … whether or not Paul has bet on a false promise and will, therefore, be put to shame for his foolish hope.'[24]

I find Stendahl's argument compelling.[25] I agree with Katherine Grieb who writes in her commentary on Romans, that it 'is a sweeping defence of the righteousness of God, the covenant faithfulness of God "to the Jew first and also to the Greek."'[26] If this point of entry to Romans is an accurate one — and I think it is — then as Thomas Long notes, its keystone passage is 1:16–17 'where Paul declares "I am not ashamed of the Gospel", a text that has long been viewed as an advance summary of the heart of the whole letter.'[27] That 'heart' is found in Romans 8.

---

[23] Krister Stendahl, *Final Account: Paul's Letter to the Romans* (Minneapolis: Fortress, 1995).

[24] Long 273.

[25] In the interest of full disclosure, I studied Matthew with him at Harvard Divinity School in the 1980s.

[26] Quoted in Long 270. And see Grieb's *The Story of Romans: A Narrative Defense of God's Righteousness* (Louisville: Westminster John Knox, 2002).

[27] Long 270.

A Brief Thematic Working Outline of Romans

1:1–17 Introductory Material treating Christology and Paul's authority

> 1:16–17 '…serves both as the climax to the introduction and the thematic statement for what follows'. (DPL 841). (Cf. Hab. 2:4; Gal. 3:11.)

1:18–3:20 The Universal State of Sin and Depravity (the 'problem' or 'illness')

> 1:18–32 among Gentiles
>
> 2:1–3:20 among Jews

3:21–23 *ALL* are sinful, BUT NOW

3:21–4:25 Divine Righteousness in Justification (the 'solution' or 'medicine')

5:1–8:30 Divine righteousness in Salvation

> Freed *from*
>
> > 5:1–21 The Power of Death
> >
> > 6:1–23 The Power of Sin
> >
> > 7:1–23 The Power of Law
>
> Freed *for*
>
> > 8:1–39 Life in the Spirit

9–11 Divine Purpose in History

12:1–15:13 *Parenesis* (Practical Exhortation/Teachings)

15:14–16:27 Extended Conclusion

ROMANS 8

There is almost universal agreement among scholars (imagine!) that Romans 8 is, in the words of Rowan Williams, 'a moment of climax' in the letter wherein 'Paul gives us one of his most wonderful and eloquent pictures of the world's possible future.' Williams continues, 'It is about a renewal of all that exists, about something entirely fresh coming to birth.'[28] Frank J. Matera, whose commentary on Romans I highly recommend, also calls Romans 8 'a climactic moment in Paul's Letter to the Romans.' He writes that:

> in chapter 8 Paul presents the new life and hope for final or eschatological glory that belongs to those who are in solidarity with Christ. … In chapter 8, he [Paul] provides … an extended discourse on the new life and hope for glory that the justified enjoy because they dwell in the sphere of God's life-giving Spirit.[29]

In addition to textual and scholarly interests, one reason I am drawn to Romans 8 is that, by describing the new creation God has inaugurated in Jesus Christ, it is a hymn to and source of hope. As does the whole of Romans, it reminds us that the way things are is neither how they were intended to be, nor how they must be. Hope often begins with envisioning alternatives to what is. In Romans 8 Paul clearly sees the 'new thing' that is in process because of Jesus Christ (8:1-17). As a practical pastor, he relates that to 'the sufferings of this present time' (8:18-26), the Spirit who 'helps us in our weakness' (8:26-27), and the promise that God is with 'those who love God, who are called according to his purpose' (8:28-39). Chapter 8 unites the

---

[28] Williams 51 and 53.

[29] Frank J. Matera, *Romans* (*Paideia* Commentaries on the NT) (Grand Rapids: Baker Academic, 2010), 185. Hereafter in text as 'Matera.'

theology with which the letter opens and the *parenesis*, the practical teaching, which follows.

The brief reflections that ensue largely follow the divisions of the Common Lectionary in year A-1. Of course there are significant studies of the place of Romans 8 in the letter as a whole and of the careful construction of the chapter itself. In particular, scholars have noted how chapter 8 echoes and develops ideas central to chapters 5 to 7.[30] Matera's commentary demonstrates how Romans 8 'brings closure' to themes in chapters 5 to 7 as follows:

8:1–4: The Spirit is the antidote
   to the power of indwelling sin described in 7:7–25.

8:5–17: The Spirit is the enabler
   of the ethical life described in 6:1–23.

8:18–39: The Spirit is the first fruits
   of the eschatological hope described in 5: 1–11.

(Matera 188)

As you make your way through Romans 8, you will find yourself accompanied by the Holy Spirit. There are some nineteen references to the Spirit in Romans 8, and for this reason alone it is important for preaching and praying. Paul asserts that because of the Holy Spirit there is no condemnation (8:1–13), no alienation (8:14–17), no 'frustration' (8:18–30), and no separation (8:31–39). (Here are four good sermon topics.) In Romans 8 Paul depicts the Holy Spirit as liberating (8:1–4), life-giving (8:9–14), and assisting (8:26–27) the Christian's 'walk', Paul's metaphor for how we live our lives. (More sermon

---

[30] Matera's schema is exceptionally clear and concise, 186–189. See also Richard J. Dillon, 'The Spirit as Taskmaster and Troublemaker in Romans 8,' *Catholic Biblical Quarterly* 60/4 (Oct 1998), 682–70; Douglas Moo, *The Epistle to the Romans* (NIC; Grand Rapids: Eerdmans, 1996).

topics.) Romans 8 immerses the reader in the activity of the Holy Spirit. And with that in mind, we turn to six practical and prayerful reflections on this most extraordinary chapter from that most extraordinary apostle.

ROMANS 8:1–11

Contrasts

1 There is therefore now no condemnation for those who are in Christ Jesus. 2 For the law of the Spirit of life in Christ Jesus has set you free from the law of sin and of death. 3 For God has done what the law, weakened by the flesh, could not do: by sending his own Son in the likeness of sinful flesh, and to deal with sin, he condemned sin in the flesh, 4 so that the just requirement of the law might be fulfilled in us, who walk not according to the flesh but according to the Spirit. 5 For those who live according to the flesh set their minds on the things of the flesh, but those who live according to the Spirit set their minds on the things of the Spirit. 6 To set the mind on the flesh is death, but to set the mind on the Spirit is life and peace. 7 For this reason the mind that is set on the flesh is hostile to God; it does not submit to God's law—indeed it cannot, 8 and those who are in the flesh cannot please God. 9 But you are not in the flesh; you are in the Spirit, since the Spirit of God dwells in you. Anyone who does not have the Spirit of Christ does not belong to him. 10 But if Christ is in you, though the body is dead because of sin, the Spirit is life because of righteousness. 11 If the Spirit of him who raised Jesus from the dead dwells in you, he who raised Christ from the dead will give life to your mortal bodies also through his Spirit that dwells in you.

Points of Interest

In *The New Interpreter's Bible,* N. T. Wright opens his commentary on the text of Romans by saying, 'The first eleven verses of Romans 8 lie at the very heart of Romans 5–8 as a whole.' They are 'tightly argued' as well as 'suffused with a sense of exultation, and celebration' (NIB 573).

The contrast between Spirit and flesh dominates the passage. As 'flesh' has been frequently misunderstood, the reflection which follows will treat its meaning and connotation. The contrast itself reflects a common teaching technique of the time, 'the two ways'. The teacher or text sets forth two opposing ideas or behaviours, the two ways, clearly intending to recommend one and denigrate the other. We know the method from Jesus' own teaching.

Musicians will remember that Romans 8:1–2 and 9–11 are the heart of one of the most frequently performed and recorded of the Bach Cantatas, *Jesu, meine Freude* (BWV 227).[31] Because it is readily available on the Internet without charge, you might wish to download it or type it into the search engine of your computer and listen to it as another *entrée* into Paul's text.

Reflection

It is a truth *almost* 'universally acknowledged', at least in the popular imagination, that the condemnatory attitude of Christians, especially toward life in the body, has put people off Christianity altogether. Nothing could be farther from the reality described at the outset of Romans 8. 'There is … no condemnation for those who are in Christ Jesus' … [who] 'has set you free from the law of sin and of death' (8:1–2). Condemnation (*katakrima*), judgment against self or others, is not for Christians. The two great problems in Greco-Roman religions, sin (*hamartias*, literally 'missing the mark') which was perhaps of special concern to Rome's Jewish Christians, and death

---

[31] It was probably written in the mid–1720s and is also known as the Motet #3 in E minor.

(*thanatou*), the 'terminal illness' to which no Gentile Greco-Roman religion spoke meaningfully, *have been solved*. In Romans 8 Paul explains that God has sent Christ Jesus who liberates the Christian, of whatever religious background or none, from both. This was made very clear in Romans 1:18–4:25 in which Paul addressed the shortcomings of *both* Gentile and Jewish Christians.

Romans 2:1 serves as a sober warning: 'Therefore you have no excuse, whoever you are, when you judge others; for in passing judgment on another you condemn yourself, because you … are doing the very same thing.' One is reminded of Jesus' statement that 'the measure you give will be the measure you get' (Matt. 7:2). Ouch! So from *where* has all this *perceived* condemnatory attitude and activity on the part of Christians originated? Well, from Christians, of course, and some of it might come from three different words in two verses: 'sinful flesh' *sarkos hamartias* (v. 3) and 'flesh-death' *sarkos thanatos* (v. 6). Is *flesh* the problem? Well, yes, it is *if* one misunderstands what Paul meant by 'flesh'. What he does not mean is what we call 'bodily life'.

In reading any passage of scripture for preaching or praying, a good first step is to be attentive to the lexical field of the text. The lexical field is the range of words the author uses, a particular root word and its variants. For example, in a text that has multiple uses of 'peace', say, 'peace' and 'peaceful' and 'peace-making', peace is likely to be the main point. Here is another example. Mark 4 has multiple uses of verbs meaning 'to hear'. So maybe what we thought was about seed or soil is really about ears (which is what Jesus explicitly *says* in 4:3, 9, 24, and 33).

The lexical field of Romans 8:1-11, actually 8:3-17, is dominated by the words 'spirit' (*pneuma/pneumatos*) and 'flesh' (*sarkos*) which are apparently used as opposites. What does Paul mean by these terms? Let's start with 'flesh.' I do not think it can mean 'corporeal body' which might be the common English denotation. Paul was, by his own admission, a highly educated and good Jew (cf. Phil. 3:4ff.). He knew the Pentateuch, knew that humankind, which God created 'in our image, according to our likeness' (Gen. 1:26), the human *body* which God created 'from the dust of the ground' (Gen 2:7), was not only good, as everything created by God was declared, but 'it was *very* good'. (Gen. 1:31, italics mine).

I would quite agree with you, if you are thinking, 'well, *good* in the biblical sense usually means something like "used for the purpose for which God intended it".' But what is created by God, and therefore intrinsically good, can be misused. (This might, but won't, lead us off into a consideration of the consequences of free will.) If God made human beings 'good', how could their 'stuff', their flesh, be intrinsically 'bad' or evil? Paul's use of 'flesh' must mean something else, and that something else is inherent in its nature or composition. 'Flesh' is impermanent.

'Little Kittel' (a theological dictionary well-known to students of *koine* Greek) has as the first definition of *sarx*/flesh '*the Muscular Part of the Body*' (italics original) which 'can also mean "meat".' As anyone who has forgotten to put the mince in the fridge knows, a chief characteristic of meat is that it rots. Indeed, the adjective derived from the Greek noun *sapros* means 'rotting' or 'decaying.' So Kittel: 'Flesh expresses human lowliness and corruptibility ...'. The *sarx* entry in Little Kittel includes a list of Paul's uses of the term. The list includes 'the whole physical existence' and '*the Earthly Sphere*' (italics in the original). It is used negatively *only* when people boast about it or put their trust in it. The Pauline section closes with the following: 'Flesh is not a separate and intrinsically bad sphere but becomes bad only with orientation to it either in licentiousness or legalism.' Flesh is 'a wrong disposition away from God', who is, of course, permanent and eternal.[32]

'Spirit', *pneuma*, is translated 'wind, breath, life.' Again, according to Little Kittel, spirit 'is a dynamic term suggesting the forceful movement of air that seizes us with elemental power and catches us up into tension or movement' (TDNT 876). Generally speaking, in the Greco-Roman world it was understood to be a divine force which had 'a mediatorial role on the border between the material and the immaterial' (TDNT 878). In the Hebrew Bible, spirit, *ru'ah*, was God's life-giving, creative, divine power, a gift to humanity. According to Schweizer, in Paul 'the *pneuma* denotes the heavenly sphere' (TDNT 888), and is 'a Sign of What Is to Come' (TDNT 889, capitals in the original). He continues, 'The antithesis of Spirit and flesh is that of divine power and human weakness (Gal. 3:2, 5)' (TDNT 890), and '*pneuma* and *sarx* represent the spheres of God and the world' (892). 'Paul contrasts the sphere of *sarx* with that of heaven or *pneuma*' (TDNT 1004).

At the outset of Romans 8 (and, indeed, in 1:3–4 at the outset of the letter) the opposite of 'flesh' is 'Spirit.' The editors of the NRSV capitalize 'spirit' when they think it refers to God or to Christ.[33] Things of the 'flesh' are negative, and things of

---

[32] E. Schweizer, '*sarx*' in G. Kittel and G. Friedrich (eds.), *Theological Dictionary of the New Testament* (Abridged in One Volume) transl. Geoffrey W. Bromiley (Grand Rapids: Eerdmans, 1985), 1000–1007. Hereafter in notes and the text as TDNT.

[33] There has been extended discussion about the Spirit and from whom it comes. (Think of the Nicean Council and subsequent creed.) In Romans 8:1–11 I tend to think 'the Spirit,' 'the Spirit of God,' and the 'spirit of Christ' are

the 'Spirit' are positive. (Recall the 'two ways' introduced above.) I suggest this is because 'fleshly things' are impermanent, and 'spiritual things' are permanent, enduring. While I am not suggesting Paul knew the words of the Johannine Jesus (Paul died long before John's Gospel was written), we might want to consider the issue here in Romans as Paul's riff on what Jesus says to the crowds and his disciples in John's Gospel: 'Do not work for the food that perishes, but for the food that endures for eternal life, which the Son of Man will give you' (John 6:27). In 2 Corinthians, Paul himself contrasts the 'outer nature' and the 'inner nature', and concludes that '… what can be seen is temporary, but what cannot be seen is eternal' (2 Cor. 4:18). (See the whole passage, 2 Corinthians 4:7–5:21, which, not coincidentally, closes by warning against judging from 'a human point of view' (5:16).)

Let me summarize: flesh is not intrinsically bad or evil. It *is* impermanent, so to direct one's life energy toward it (and its realm) *is* deathly. Spirit is a perceptible manifestation of the Divine, of God or of Christ. If 'flesh' is a metaphor for what is perishable, 'spirit' is a metaphor for what is imperishable. Think of 1 Corinthians 15:35–50, especially verses 42–45 which begin, 'What is sown is perishable, what is raised is imperishable.' Paul wants the Roman Christians to live 'according to' or 'in the direction of' Spirit rather than flesh, because 'flesh is death', i.e. impermanent, and Spirit, being of

---

used, if not synonymously, at least interchangeably. Each is eternal, imperishable. But see John R. Coulson, 'Jesus and the Spirit in Paul's Theology: The Earthly Jesus', *Catholic Biblical Quarterly* 79/1 (Jan., 2017), 77–96; and on that troubling phrase in 8:3, Florence Morgan Gillman, 'Another look at Romans 8:3: "In the Likeness of Sinful Flesh,"' *Catholic Biblical Quarterly* 49/4 (Oct. 1987), 597–604. Her conclusion is that Christ did not sin but 'was involved in the same power sphere of unredeemed existence as other humans, that he bore the identical sin-prone flesh that humans have.' Paul was 'articulating a total identity between Christ and other humans …', 604.

God and of the resurrected Christ, is permanent.[34] *And,* as an experience, Spirit is *given,* gratuitous, a gift, and thus universally available to those willing to accept it. Of course, a gift is only actually so when the recipient receives or accepts it.

Paul assumes that the Roman Christians 'are not in the flesh' — he cannot mean they are not living in the body or he could not be writing and sending a letter by means of the very real Phoebe — 'you are in the Spirit, since the Spirit of God dwells in you' (8:9). They received that Spirit when they were 'baptized into Christ Jesus' (6:3). The One who raised Christ from the dead, gives life to their 'mortal bodies' (a rather limp translation of *ta thanata somata,* 'the subject-to-death bodies') through the Spirit's indwelling (8:11). That which is imperishable inhabits the perishable, which is why 'There is ... no condemnation for those who are in Christ Jesus' (8:1). And *nobody* can boast about it, because the whole thing is gift, God's doing (8:3, 11). Dunn puts it this way:

> Those who have received the Spirit of Christ ... have a completely other 'base of operations' than simply the flesh. It is from that base that they must live and act. They must live out the reality ... which they already experience through the Spirit and share with God's son.
>
> (Rom 8:1-17, DPL 847)

In a reflection on the Spirit in Romans 8:1-11 some years ago, Professor John Knox of Union Seminary wrote, '"The

---

[34] Distinguished Paul scholar, Richard J. Dillon, has a very different view. He views flesh 'as the sphere of influence generated by human ungodliness, the "house" in which Sin comfortably resides.' '... the modes of existence "according to the flesh" and "according to the spirit" are distinguished by opposite goals or policies of human conduct ...' 'The Spirit as Taskmaster and Troublemaker in Romans 8,' *Catholic Biblical Quarterly* 60/4 (Oct 1998), 689 and 693.

Spirit" is another way of referring to the quality, the substance, the experienced reality of the life in Christ.' He continues:

> The Spirit is God's own presence, his very being surrounding us and pervading us, his own love encompassing us and possessing us, and wanting to possess us utterly. ... [T]he spirit which we receive ... we also experience as the Spirit of Christ, the actual presence among us, with us and within us, of the Lord Jesus himself.[35]

Knox argues that 'the opposition between "flesh" and "Spirit" is not primarily 'an idea or conception, but a concrete, a felt, reality' (Knox 83).

This is an arresting insight. It means that Romans 8 opens not only with a theological explanation of the Holy Spirit, but with the *experiential* reality of it, the reality of God's gift, through the resurrection of Jesus Christ, of an *enlivening* of flesh, life in 'mortal bodies' through the indwelling Spirit. This is very similar to the idea in Colossians that God 'has rescued us from the power of darkness and transferred us into the kingdom of his beloved Son' (Col. 1:13). Paul opens his letter to the Roman Christians by asking them to take stock of their own experience of freedom and life and peace *received* (not manufactured or earned) through what God has done in Christ. Jew or Gentile, this is God's gift to them. God wants them to experience it. Indeed, N. T. Wright notes that even in 'the great logic of Romans 5–8, love is not an idea to be worked out, but a fact, an experienced fact ...' (NIB 10:609).

---

[35] John Knox, *Life in Christ Jesus: Reflections on Romans 5–8* (New York: The Seabury Press, 1966), 74, 75 and 76. Hereafter in the text as Knox.

In an essay entitled 'Spirituality as Common Sense' the beloved Benedictine spiritual teacher, Brother David Steindl-Rast wrote:

> What you don't know from your own experience, you just don't know. Therefore, you have to start from your own experience, and my experience tells me that when I am fully alive … when my body blazes … then I also belong to God… [36]

It is this full aliveness, this belonging, which is offered to the whole person by the Spirit as gift, as concrete, felt reality, as the well-spring of joy and life and community with the myriad other children and heirs of God. The next unit of Romans will address this extraordinary, family reality.

For Prayer and Pondering

1. What, for you, are the actual connections between your 'fleshly' life and your 'spirituality'? What is the rapport between your body and the life of the Spirit which, by virtue of your baptism, indwells you?

2. How does the fact that 'there is … no condemnation for those who are in Christ Jesus' affect your attitudes toward others? Your own tendency to judge others, especially other Christians? If you have no such tendency, you are an immediate candidate for canonization!

---

[36] Br David Steindl-Rast, OSB, 'Spirituality as Common Sense', *The Quest* 3/2 (Summer, 1990) quoted in *David Steindl-Rast: Essential Writings*, selected by Clare Hallward (Maryknoll, NY: Orbis Books, 2010), 50.

ROMANS 8:12-17
Trinity Sunday

Liturgical Note

Romans 8:12–17 is the text appointed for Trinity Sunday, the first Sunday after Pentecost/Whitsun, a commemoration not widely observed until the Middle Ages. The feast became popular in England, perhaps because St Thomas Becket was consecrated bishop on that Sunday in 1162. Beginning in the later Middle Ages, in the Sarum Missal (and now in the Book of Common Prayer) Sundays are counted from Trinity Sunday. Trinity Sunday is intended to highlight the three Persons of the Trinity, 'God in Three Persons', now 'completed' by the coming of the Spirit on Pentecost. In some ways, Trinity Sunday fulfils the liturgical movement from Passion to Easter to Pentecost. It is the last of the 'big Sundays'. Palm Sunday, Easter, Ascension forty days later, ten days after *that* Pentecost, and then Trinity Sunday which is the 'hinge' between the Christian 'high holy days' and 'ordinary time' — as if *any* time were ordinary! Holy Week, Easter, Ascension, Pentecost *are* the 'Trinity Story', but are so dramatic in and of themselves that we might miss their Trinitarian aspect. So we get a Sunday to pay attention.

12 So then, brothers and sisters, we are debtors, not to the flesh, to live according to the flesh— 13 for if you live according to the flesh, you will die; but if by the Spirit you put to death the deeds of the body, you will live. 14 For all who are led by the Spirit of God are children of God. 15 For you did not receive a spirit of slavery to fall back into fear, but you have received a spirit of adoption. When we cry, 'Abba! Father!' 16 it is that very Spirit bearing witness with our spirit that we

are children of God, 17 and if children, then heirs, heirs of God and joint heirs with Christ — if, in fact, we suffer with him so that we may also be glorified with him.

Points of Interest

The text opens in 8:12 with a firm assertion: 'So then', *Ara oun*. What follows comes from what preceded. It continues the flesh/Spirit comparison in 8:1–11, and in verses 12–13 offers a stark choice between them. Verse 14 introduces the new and surprising idea that if we live by, are led by, the Spirit of God, we are children of God[37]. The language of slaves in chapters 6 and 7 now becomes the language of children and siblings and marks a remarkable transition. As Matera's commentary notes, 'in contrasting a Spirit of adoption with a spirit of slavery, Paul is emphasizing the distinctive nature of the Spirit that believers have received ...' (Matera 198).

The language of domination (slavery) moves toward that of familial affection, *Abba*. Those for whom *Abba/Father* language is difficult, or those who preach to them, might wish to read up a bit on the connotation of the Aramaic *Abba* which Jesus both uses and commends to His disciples. Joachim Jeremias (whom no one, to my knowledge, has called a feminist), opens *The Prayers of Jesus* with what is still one of the best discussions of *Abba*: 'For Orientals, the word "Father" as applied to God ... encompasses from earliest times, something of what the word "Mother" signifies among us.'[38] Rather than the domineering

---

[37] One wonders why the editors of the NRSV did not capitalize 'spirit' in 'spirit of adoption' in v. 15 or in 'our spirit' in v. 16, since, in essence, the Christian's spirit is God's.

[38] Chapter 1, *Abba*, in Joachim Jeremias, *The Prayers of Jesus* (Philadelphia: Fortress, 1967).

and masculine, father-language is to evoke the familiarity, nurture, and safety of the healthy family.

Reflection

The following is, more or less, the Trinity's story: In the beginning, God created. For a long time, the First Person of the Trinity, God the Father, the Creator 'of all that is, seen and unseen' as the Creed has it, seems to work alone (with Wisdom alongside). God creates the world and calls a family to be His representatives and, later, gives them a pattern to live by. Like most families, this chosen one does not always follow the rules or get along too well together. So God sends special people, prophets, to remind them of God's original intention. Finally, maybe at least in part in exasperation, God gets in a 'don't make me come down there' mode, but does, in fact, come down here.

Enter the Second Person of the Trinity, God the Son, the Redeemer. Amazingly, in Jesus, God takes on human limitation in 'the likeness of sinful flesh' (8:3), and yet never transgresses God's original intention for how things ought to be. Unfortunately, a number of people did not, and do not, care too much for Jesus' explanation of God's plan for God's *basilea*, God's 'kingdom' or 'reign'. So the Second Person of the Trinity got in trouble, especially with religious authorities. No surprise there. But before things came to a grisly head at Golgatha, Jesus promised those who *did*, and do, get it, who do want to live as the First Person of the Trinity intended, special help, a 'secret weapon' whom, in His 'Farewell Discourse' to His disciples in John's Gospel (chapters 13–17) Jesus calls the Comforter, or Advocate or Paraclete, depending on the translation. Each translation is a good one because from time to time we all need comfort or someone to speak up for us or an 'alongsider'.

The Second Person of the Trinity is 'crucified, died and buried,' and in one of the First Person's biggest surprises, 'raised on the third day'. Then, for forty days the Second Person lives his First Person life among humans. But in order for the Third Person to come, the Second Person has to go away. Just before He is taken up to heaven He says 'I am sending upon you what my father promised; so stay here ... until you have been clothed with power from on high' (Luke 24:49). 'You will receive power when the Holy Spirit has come upon you' (Acts 1:8). As promised, 'when the day of Pentecost had come' (2:1),' all of them were filled with the Holy Spirit ...' (Acts 2:5). The Spirit who is to be with them (and us) forever (John 14:16), will teach us everything and remind us of what Jesus said (John 14:26), will testify on Jesus' behalf (John 15:26), prove 'the world' (the opponents of the Second Person) wrong (John 16:8), and guide believers into all truth (John 16:12). And so, according to the Nicene Creed, on Pentecost, after the Second Person has ascended, the First and Second Persons of the Trinity send the Third Person of the Trinity, the Holy Spirit, the Sustainer of all that Person One and Person Two accomplished. Whew!

In spite of the good work of historical Christian theology, I readily confess I do not understand how one can be three, or the exact relationship of each of the Three Persons of the One God to each of the others. I leave the exact explanations to the St Thomas Aquinases of the faith. But in a rather simple-minded, practical sense, I think the Trinity suggests that God is not so much 'object' or 'person', in the sense that you and I are persons, as *relationship*, the energy, synergy and/or activity of loving relationship. The whole Trinitarian story of creating and redeeming creation, sustaining its being (that is, keeping it in existence) and effecting its redemption, is a love story.

That is why these four verses from Romans are appointed for Trinity Sunday. In them Paul radically departs from the language of slaves and captivity in chapters 6 and 7 (6:16–20; 7:6, 14, 25), and moves to the language of parent, children, and heirs in chapter 8. In this context, I am reminded of the words of Jesus in John 15:15: 'I do not call you servants, [*doulou*, literally 'slaves'] any longer. … I have called you friends.' Parents create children (and heirs) in love. The family is to be a unit of love. In the Romans' socio-political context, the familial metaphor is powerful, and echoes Trinitarian ideas.

Paul addresses the Roman Christians as *adelphoi*, brethren, that is family members (8:12), and writes that *all*, not just Jews or only Gentiles, who are led by the Spirit of God (Third Person here proceeding from First Person) are children of God (8:14). This is a big turn, the *peripatea*, in the Trinity's story, because heretofore God's children were chosen from a particular family. But now *all*, not just the original blood line, can be God's children. As the Ephesian letter puts it, the Second Person 'has broken down the dividing wall' (Eph. 2:14). Ephesians 2:11–22 is, in fact, a wonderful gloss on this passage.

Paul's implied comparison in the initial chapters of Romans is between slaves and children. Slaves and children were, of course, both members of a Greco-Roman household, and both were at the low end of its hierarchy, as we see in the 'household codes' of Ephesians 5:21–6:9 and of Colossians 3:18–4:1. But only children could inherit. Paul's point is that through the 'given' spirit of adoption, *all* are children of God (Person One). Adoption is 'conferred', given; the children are specially *chosen*. 'Free children are heirs who can hope for an inheritance' (Matera 198). As Richard Carlson writes in his notes on preaching Romans 8:12–17:

This use of adoption imagery combines the Greco-Roman legal concept of adoption and the Jewish concept of Israel's election as God's child. An adopted child is one whose identity, status, and relationships are now determined by belonging to the family.[39]

These children, the ones by blood and the ones by adoption, are both heirs to all that is God's. Imagine *that* for a moment.

In fact, it is through the Spirit (Person Three) that one can address God (Person One) as 'Abba! Father!', can address God as Jesus, Himself (Person Two), did. As Rowan Williams notes, 'The Spirit of God comes alive in us so that we are able to say Jesus' own words, "Abba, Father" ...'.[40] The Spirit gives the gift of this mode of address, and it is the proof or witness that we *are* in fact God's children, in the intimate relationship of child to parent that occurs in a healthy family (8:14-15). The language of children and heirs must have sounded both shocking and very sweet in the ears of the Roman Christians. Some of them were undoubtedly slaves who could not inherit anything. Some of them must have lost their biological family connections when they 'decided to follow Jesus' as the old Gospel hymn puts it. Some of them must have been orphans. It was not only the name of Jesus that sounded sweet in their ears, but the knowledge that they were co-heirs with him. *AND*, if we are *all* God's children, which we are, and heirs of Christ, which we are, then we are siblings of one another, in a familial relationship with every other Christian to whom we owe the same responsibilities and the same love that we do to biological siblings. Imagine *that* for a moment, too.

---

[39] Richard P. Carlson, 'Romans 8:12-17,' *Interpretation* 58/2 (July 2004), 281.
[40] Williams 67.

Trinity Sunday is about live and potent relationships: the persons of the Trinity to each other, ours to the Persons of the Trinity, ours to each other. Through the redemption effected by Jesus (Person Two), we become children of God (Person One), and are empowered by the Holy Spirit (Person Three of the God Triad) to continue in relationship to the One God. The activity of the Trinity makes us children cared for by an extraordinary Parent, siblings to an extraordinary Brother, and heirs with Him to something promised which we did not in any way earn or deserve (just as I did nothing to earn the legacy left me by my father; he gave it to me because I was his daughter, and he loved me). The Trinity story is a story of amazing grace that has made us, redeemed us, and will sustain us until we return home to our Maker and Divine Parent.

In his reflection on this text John Knox makes much of the idea of home. He suggests that 'Our most deeply felt need is our need of home.' 'Our malady is not our ignorance, or even our weakness, but our homesickness. What we all most deeply need is … an environment of relationships …' (Knox 94 and 96). Knox reminds us that 'however far we may have wandered from the Father's house, we are still his children — created in his image, objects of his care — and repentance is a returning to a status and a relationship which belong to our true nature and which we can never altogether lose' (Knox 94). Thus the preacher might bring Jesus' parable of the 'Prodigal Son' in Luke 15:1–32 (which is really the story of the Prodigal — in quite another way — Father) to bear on this text in Romans.

The following story came to me on the internet some ten years ago. I do not remember from whom or its source: A man was on a long airline flight. His seat mate was a little girl. Well into the flight the 'fasten seatbelt' sign came on, and the voice came over the loudspeaker 'we won't be serving you beverages as we are expecting turbulence. Please check the security of your seat belt.' Naturally, people began to be a bit apprehensive, and more so when the same voice announced 'We are sorry to be unable to serve you a meal. The turbulence is still ahead of us.' Not a comforting announcement.

They flew into the storm of thunder and lightning, and the plane bounced around like a cork in the heavens. It was terrible. People clutched their seats and each other's hands. Fear was palpable. And through it all, the little girl read her book, seemingly oblivious to danger. Her small world seemed calm. As the plane was buffeted by the storm, lurched, rose and fell, as the adults were scared to death, she was composed and unafraid. Her seat mate could hardly take his eyes off that child. Happily, the plane did safely reach its destination. As passengers hurried to disembark, the man spoke to the little girl who had been so serene in the storm. He asked her why she had not been afraid. She replied, 'Sir, my dad is the pilot, and he is taking me home.'

'For all who are led by the Spirit of God are children of God' (Rom. 8:14), the God who is a loving relationship of Three Persons, the God who is the ultimate pilot in all storms, and who is, with help from Persons Two and Three, taking us all safely home.

For Prayer and Pondering

1. How does my experience of my own family of origin affect or colour how I read Paul's family language (for example 'Father', 'children', 'sibling', 'adopted')?

2. In our lives of prayer we tend to be *Theocentric* (First Person) or *Christocentric* (Second Person) or *Pneumacentric* (Third Person). Which are you? And how might exploring the 'other Persons' encourage growth in your prayer life?

ROMANS 8:18–23
Suffering

18 I consider that the sufferings of this present time are not worth comparing with the glory about to be revealed to us. 19 For the creation waits with eager longing for the revealing of the children of God; 20 for the creation was subjected to futility, not of its own will but by the will of the one who subjected it, in hope 21 that the creation itself will be set free from its bondage to decay and will obtain the freedom of the glory of the children of God. 22 We know that the whole creation has been groaning in labour pains until now; 23 and not only the creation, but we ourselves, who have the first fruits of the Spirit, groan inwardly while we wait for adoption, the redemption of our bodies.

Points of Interest

This passage is linked to the preceding with the connective particle *gar*, for, the same particle which causes so much *angst* at the end of Mark 16:8. Paul closed the preceding section of the letter with the reminder that children and heirs of God, as was Jesus, are still subject to suffering. 'Suffer with', *sumpaschomen* (8:17), introduces the subject of suffering, *pathemata* (8:18), which is the focus in this, the second section of Romans 8. Readers will hear in it echoes of 2 Corinthians 4:17–18. But what is in view here is not only the suffering of individual believers, but of 'the whole creation' (8:22). Note the pattern of the passage is from the human (v. 18) to the cosmic (vv. 19–22) to the human (vv. 23–25). Dillon points out that 'the status of offspring and heirs is modified by an essential condition: "if

37

indeed we suffer with him so as also to be glorified with him." That brief clause ... is really the hinge which coordinates the argument of the two sections 8:12–17 and 8:18–30.'[41]

Reflection

Life in the Spirit sets one free from slavery to sin and death. It does not exempt one from suffering. Christians of the first century knew a good deal about suffering. The church to which Paul is writing will, very shortly, live under the thumb of the cruel and crazy Emperor Nero who blamed Christians for the great fire in Rome in AD 64 and persecuted them mercilessly. In Paul's time, when Romans became Christians they lost many privileges of citizenship (if they were citizens) as Christianity was *religio illicita*. They may also have lost favour and connection with their biological families. Paul himself knew a good deal about suffering as autobiographical references indicate (cf. 2 Cor. 11:21b–12:10, Phil. 1:12–26 and 3:4b–11).[42] Everyone has always lived under the spectre of what Shakespeare called 'the slings and arrows of outrageous fortune' (*Hamlet* III.I).

In the midst of this discussion of suffering it is as if Paul raises his gaze beyond the present and the trials of the individual and sees the whole cosmos from the perspective of eternity. What he glimpses and attempts to communicate is the connectedness of the whole created universe and the intrinsic value of physical life to God's plan of redemption. 'Creation' (*ktisis*, from the verb *ktizo*, 'to make') was a term with a long history in Greco-Roman philosophy and Hebrew scripture. It

---

[41] Dillon 697.
[42] A helpful overview of Paul's thinking about suffering is Scott J. Hafemann, 'Suffering', DPL, 919–921.

meant 'the totality of created things' and, therefore, God's creative work as a whole (TDNT 484).[43]

Paul begins with a hard-headed look at present reality. The present situation is not good, and it is not only human beings who are suffering. Paul's vision expands the human predicament to the whole physical universe. The creation itself is 'subjected to futility' (v. 20) and 'groaning in labour pains' (v. 22), a more graphic translation than 'travail'. The Greek word translated 'futility' means 'aimlessness', not achieving the goal for which something was created. We might say the creation was not living up to its potential. It cries out in the pains of childbirth, a vivid and vital picture of what precedes new life. Paul, who is sometimes unjustly accused of misogyny, describes the suffering of creation in terms of a woman in childbirth labouring to bring forth a new kind of life.

This situation is part of a larger plan which has always been under God's control. Paul says the creation suffers, not by its own choice or will, (it is not masochistic), but 'by the will of the one who subjected it', by God. What?!? Commentators suggest that here Paul has in view Genesis 3:17 when God curses the ground. Due to Adam's sin (yes, a choice), creation has fallen under God's judgment. The Fall led to suffering, but is also the source of hope. Since God is the source of judgment, God is also the source of the solution. *Felix culpa*, indeed. Even in suffering, all of creation is subject to God.

The whole world is, indeed, in God's hands. N. T. Wright argues persuasively that:

The covenant between God and Israel was established in the first place … to deal with the problem of the world as

---

[43] For an overview see Foerster's article in TDNT, 481–486 and J. R. Levison, 'Creation and New Creation' in DPL, 189–190.

a whole. ... The covenant ... was established so that the creator God could rescue the creation from evil, corruption, and disintegration and ... could rescue humans from sin and death. [God's justice] is setting to rights that which is out of joint, restoring things as they should be. (NIB 10:399)

Looking back to v. 18, this is why in the midst of human suffering, apparent aimlessness, and travail both human and cosmic, Paul can speak of glory and redemption. No matter how great the suffering, it is insignificant in the face of the FACT of the glory to be revealed to (and in) believers. It is precisely at the point of suffering that God reckons (Barth's word) with us, as, indeed, God reckoned with Paul when God did *not* remove the 'thorn ... in the flesh', but gave him something better, grace sufficient. 'My grace is sufficient for you, for power (other translations read 'my power') is made perfect in weakness' (2 Cor. 12:9). 'Therefore I am content with weaknesses, insults, hardships, persecutions, and calamities for the sake of Christ; for whenever I am weak, then I am strong,' Paul tells the Corinthians (2 Cor. 12:10).[44] Perhaps on the basis of this earlier experience, here in Romans 8 Paul, in an incredible flash of insight, insists that we shall recover within ourselves the divine image that was lost at the Fall. In light of the recovery of that image in us — 'the hope of glory' as Colossians 1:27 states, or Christ's 'Spirit that dwells in you' (Rom. 8:11) — all else pales.

Paul is absolutely sure of this because the Roman Christians, and we ourselves, already have 'the first-fruits of the Spirit' (v. 23, and the subject of vv. 1–17). In Jewish tradition, first-fruits of the harvest were offered to God as pledge of the

---

[44] This is another image of the great Pascal Mystery: at the point of our Lord's greatest weakness, degradation, and death, God's 'reckoning' kicked in, and the redemption, the re-creation of all creation began.

whole harvest. (See, for example, Lev. 23:9–14; Num. 18:13–18; Deut. 8:4.) For 'first-fruits' Paul uses the word *aparche* which:

> was often used also in the sense of 'earnest money, a guarantee of what was still to be paid, of what was to come.' The Spirit has been given ... as a down-payment that guarantees that the rest will come in due course, i.e. glory in the presence of the Father.[45]

Here, the Holy Spirit, which we have now in part, is a pledge of our final salvation. As G. M. Burge notes, 'The Spirit serves to reassure and sustain believers as God's partial gift of the whole of salvation awaiting them' (DPL 301). This idea seems to have been fairly common in the early church. The author of James writes, 'In fulfilment of [God's] own purpose he gave us birth by the word of truth, so that we would become a kind of first fruits (*aparchen*) of his creatures' (1:18). Writing to the church at Corinth Paul put it this way: '... God ... has given us the Spirit as a guarantee' (2 Cor. 5:5). The Spirit is the down-payment assuring the full realization of our inheritance as the sons and daughters of God.

This inheritance is not just a spiritualized abstraction. Paul conceives of it in terms of the 'redemption of our bodies' (v. 23), the freedom from decay and corruption which all created things also await. The body, *somatos*, included those impermanent, 'fleshly' bodies that figured in 8:1–17. Why bodies? Because our bodies, corporeal and incorporeal, are our connection to the physical world, to the other 'stuff' that God has made. The stuff of the universe, the stuff of the cosmos is our stuff.

---

[45] Joseph A. Fitzmyer, SJ, *Spiritual Exercises Based on Paul's Epistle to the Romans* (New York: Paulist Press, 1995), 139.

Looking beyond the present moment of individual suffering, Paul has an insight of universal and eternal consequence. Dillon articulates it clearly: '... Paul raises the plane of the discourse from the community of faith to the cosmos at large.'[46] His Jewish theological training included a vision and hope for a new creation. In the great hymn of Isaiah 65:17-25 by the mouth of the prophet God announced:

For I am about to create new heavens and a new earth;
the former things shall not be remembered or come to mind.
But be glad and rejoice forever in what I am creating ...

(vv. 17-18)

Paul sees in the redemption brought about by the death and resurrection of Jesus the beginning of that new creation. Earlier he had written, '... if anyone is in Christ, there is a new creation: everything old has passed away; see, everything has become new!' (2 Cor. 5:17). The consequences of the Fall, in which human over-reaching affected the whole creation, are erased by the generous self-giving of Jesus. Those who have joined themselves to Him in baptism (been buried and resurrected with him as per Rom. 6:3-11), have entered into the new creation Jesus initiated.[47] And *through them/us* there is hope for the whole created universe. The redemption of human beings and their/our experience of the Holy Spirit are grounds for hope for the whole universe. There is suffering to be endured, but glory beyond it (8:17).

The *experience* of the Holy Spirit is, in Paul's view, critical. Matera notes that 'if contemporary believers find ... Pauline teaching foreign, the fault does not lie so much with the

---

[46] Dillon 698.
[47] For a short introduction to 'New Creation' and excellent suggestions for further reading see J. R. Levison, DPL, 189-190.

apostle's theology as it does with *the absence of an experience of the Spirit* that often characterizes contemporary Christianity.' He goes on to reflect that this experience of the Spirit accounts for the rapid growth and energy of the early church, and its 'absence accounts for the malaise that afflicts much of contemporary Christianity' (Matera 210, italics in the original).

The familiar configuration of our current problems was perhaps beyond Paul's imagination. Although he might not recognize the terms 'racism' or 'sexism' he knew their reality as the shocking assertion of Galatians 3:28 indicates. Paul might not recognize the phrases 'arms race', ecological crisis', 'climate change', 'sustainable agriculture' or 'holistic urban planning', but he had a cosmic world view in which the solution to these and many other problems was already in process. In it, human life and the life of the universe are intrinsically bound together, and the hope for the whole of creation is found in the redemption begun in Jesus Christ. Although it is that, the resurrection of Jesus is about much more than me and my individual salvation. The world itself and human life are linked, if by nothing else, by their mutual groaning in travail, their straining toward the future new creation present in that very suffering. Behind suffering, apparent frustration, futility, and aimlessness is the vision of a harmonious universe ordered by a benevolent God. It is a universe with rough edges, to be sure, but it is one beatified throughout all eternity by God's continuing to whisper to it 'good, good, very good' and by becoming incarnate to demonstrate how good it *could* be.

Although they come from different theological perspectives and the temporal metaphors they employ are apparently at odds, the very different contemporary Christian thinkers, Philip Yancy and Rowan Williams, both have profoundly understood Paul's cosmic vision. Yancy said in an interview 'I don't have much hope on a global scale, but on a cosmic scale I believe God will intervene rather dramatically when Jesus returns. In the meantime, my hope rests in small groups of Christians around the world showing what God had in mind.'[48] In *Meeting God in Paul*, Williams has written:

> God's future is alive here and now, and it is us. We who are living in the Christian community are living *on the other side of the end of the world*, living in God's life — to which the whole life of the universe is being drawn, not in an irresistible natural process but by a timeless and unchanging love seeking to reconcile or heal what is broken in the created world at every level.
>
> (69, italics in the original)

Suffering is real and sometimes very, very terrible. Nobody will convince me otherwise. Perhaps an expansive Pauline vision of redeemed creation is cold comfort in a particular instance of suffering. It is not what I would reach for pastorally when called to the ICU of the hospital, for instance. But for me at least, it is a great, if peculiar, encouragement if in the midst of suffering I can remember, catch even the most fleeting glimpse of the fact, that by it and how I bear it, I might assist in bringing to birth the new creation begun on Calvary and seen by the women at the empty tomb. It might give me a deeper, more existential understanding of how all suffering is mysteriously given meaning in the Cross of Christ. The challenge of this text in Romans for preaching and prayer is to raise our eyes above the common round, the specific, temporal circumstances, and glimpse Paul's cosmic vision: God with the whole world and all of history in His hands.

---

[48] Charles E. Moore, 'The Weapons of Grace' (interview with Philip Yancy), *The Plough Quarterly* (Winter, 2016), 53.

For Prayer and Pondering

1. How does Paul's view of suffering in Romans 8 enlighten (or darken) your own understanding and experience of suffering?

2. What practical 'preaching points' might there be between any of our current, corporate sufferings (ecological crises, racism, etc.) and Paul's cosmic vision of redemption?

ROMANS 8:24-25
Hope

24 For in hope we were saved. Now hope that is seen is not hope. For who hopes for what is seen? 25 But if we hope for what we do not see, we wait for it with patience.

Points of Interest

In Romans Paul has already linked suffering and hope: '… we also boast in our sufferings, knowing that suffering produces endurance, and endurance produces character, and character produces hope, and hope does not disappoint us, because God's love has been poured into our hearts through the Holy Spirit that has been given to us' (5:3-4). These verses colour the material in Chapter 8. Many translations of Romans and commentaries on it suggest 8:24-25 is the conclusion of 8:18-25, and there are good reasons for doing so. There is practical, pastoral, and psychological wisdom in closing a consideration of suffering with hope. And, in fact, vv. 26-30 also ameliorate the discussion of suffering by reminding the reader that 'the Spirit helps us' and that 'all things work together for good for those who love God.' The remainder of chapter 8 seems intended to encourage sufferers. And, of course, suffering is ubiquitous. Everyone suffers. As a caveat, John Knox reminds us 'There is a distinctively Christian way of bearing the ordinary sufferings … but the sufferings themselves are distinctively Christian only when they are voluntarily incurred and endured for the sake of Christ' (Knox 102).

'Who can be alive…without feeling the imminent threat of despair?' queries Knox, and continues '… we struggle finally, not against flesh and blood, but against dark powers in the soul, whose assaults do not depend upon the changing circumstances of history or the shifts in our outward fortunes' (Knox 104). As Paul in Romans has understood sin as a power, so Knox sees despair as a 'dark power'. Because hopelessness and despair are perennial human challenges, I have singled out these two verses for a brief consideration on hope by introducing its etymology, Paul's view of it, and some suggestions about how one might maintain or nurture hope in hard times.

Reflection

Perhaps paradoxically, it seems that the suffering of those Roman believers was *because of* their faith in Christ. The children and heirs of God suffer *with* Christ 'so that [they] may be glorified with him' (8:17). In his article on the Spirit in Romans 8, Dillon asserts:

> The suffering of believers in the present situation is … the *result* of their possession of the Spirit as first-fruits and does not belie it. …The Spirit not only brings bliss and contentment but … acts as an unsettling corrective force. This is one side of the Spirit's coin; on the other is the Spirit's role as supporter and beatifier of the faithful.
> (699 & 702, italics in original)

N. T. Wright agrees: 'Suffering comes as a result of the Gospel, which, by its announcement of Jesus as Lord, challenges all other lordships, many of which, at both the cosmic and the terrestrial levels, will fight in defence' (NIB 10: 617). Christians need hope in their suffering because, by virtue of their *being* Christians and having received the Spirit, they *will* suffer.

The Greek word 'hope' (*elpis*, and the verb form *elpizo*, to hope) has a long, philosophical history. Plato thought human life was not merely about acceptance of the present and

47

remembering the past, but about expectations for the future. 'Hopes are subjective projections of the future' (TDNT 229). For Plato they could be positive or negative, good or bad, or neutral. In Hebrew scripture, on the other hand 'Hope is expectation of good'. ... 'The life of the righteous is grounded in a hope that implies a future because its point of reference is God' (TDNT 230).

On the basis of God's faithfulness in the past, God's *hesed* or loving-kindness, Jews trusted what God would do in the future. The challenge, then, was to wait and to trust. As J. M. Everts explains, 'Because God is the hope of the righteous they can expect good things from God and wait patiently for his help and deliverance' (DPL 415). It is as the Psalmist declares, '... I will hope continually,/and will praise you yet more and more' (71:14). Furthermore, present hope in God is also hope in the future when God will intervene for the righteous. The understanding that the future belonged to God influenced both Messianic expectation and the hope for the eschatological restoration of Israel in the Hellenistic period and the time of Jesus.

The New Testament understanding of hope is deeply rooted in the soil of the Hebrew Bible and Jewish expectation. We hear this clearly in the opening verses of the Book of Hebrews (1:1–4) and in Hebrews 11:1–2 and following. 'The main difference from the Old Testament is that the act of salvation has now been accomplished in Christ' (TDNT 213). Everts suggests that 'Paul understands Christian hope as a fulfilment of God's promises to Israel.' That hope is anchored in Israel's history and 'in the revealed character of God as one who is faithful to his promises' (DPL 415). Romans 8:24–25 assumes that hope depends on the salvation accomplished in Christ, not visibly present (which would make it material, *sarx-*

48

like, and therefore impermanent). 'The Christian faith lives from the raising of Christ from the dead and strains toward the hope of a future given by God' (DPL 417). So Christian hope requires patient endurance;[49] '... we wait for it with patience' (8:25).

Some years ago I had the opportunity to think seriously about keeping hope alive in challenging times, an exercise in patient endurance. A friend at the local Jesuit College asked if I would give a talk on hope for a novena for peace that the students were having. It was a big challenge for all of us, in part because it was less than a year after 9/11. My first response was to say, 'no; sorry'. I was not feeling at all hopeful. But, not too enthusiastically, I said OK, and that led me to an important attitude adjustment.

My distress was not just about the events of 9/11, but about the responses to it. It was terrible to join the thousands of innocent people in the world who have been victims of terrorism, or experienced its aftermath, to witness so much suffering. But the official response was horrible in kind. We began our own bombing programme against a people we now know were largely innocent. We were sabre rattling in a way that is terrifying in a nuclear world. Not even Christians wanted to hear the words of the innocent victim of political violence, Jesus of Nazareth, as he was being nailed to the cross, 'Father, forgive them; for they do not know what they are doing' (Luke 23:34). Nor were people anxious to hear the words of Paul to the suffering church in Rome, 'Do not repay anyone evil for evil ...' (12:17). It seemed ridiculous to talk about hope,

---

[49] My summary depends heavily on the material in the entry on *elpis* in TDNT 229–232 and on 'Hope' in DPL 415–417.

but the *students* were praying for peace, so I turned to Romans 8:22–25 and began to think about what *gives* me hope.

First, I remembered that I am not the only one who suffers. Everyone does. Indeed, 'the whole creation', people, plants, animals, everything God created, is groaning in labour pains, groaning toward the dawn of a better day and a better way that God has in store. There is an odd comfort in the solidarity of suffering. Others suffer, too, and have survived it. I might. You might. There is hope.

Second, 'hope that is seen is not hope' (8:24). Hope is a *desire* for something accompanied by the *expectation* that it is attainable. If one 'has it' or 'sees it', it is fulfilment or attainment, not hope. Certainly the call of God to the faithful in terrible times (personal, corporate, or cosmic) is to maintain hope *in spite of* the current circumstances, to trust at darkest midnight that dawn is coming. Especially for the Christian, hope keeps us from being mired in the present. It propels us toward the future, which is God's.

Third, in his extraordinary book *He Leadeth Me* about the spiritual lessons he learned in twenty-three years in Soviet prisons and slave-labour camps, Fr. Walter Ciszek SJ says that the greatest gift God can give is to send a person a trial that person *cannot* bear with his or her own power, and then to sustain him or her with grace to endure *in* that trial. In absolute powerlessness in the face of suffering, one must surrender oneself to God, abandon oneself to Divine Providence (to allude to another Jesuit, the eighteenth-century Jean-Pierre de Caussade), however silent and absent it seems. Something about the surrender itself can open the way for one's own experience of 'My grace is sufficient for you, for power is made perfect in weakness' (2 Cor. 12:9). Perhaps to wait patiently for what we do not see is always God's assignment for the faithful in intractable suffering.

Fourth, what does one do practically while hoping for what cannot yet bet seen? For me at least the answer has to do with deriving strength from what I *can* see. Hope is tied to gratitude for what is, the sometimes challenging attempt to find the gift in all that is around me. I maintain what hope I have by the giftedness of daily life. I have a safe and quiet place to live. Fresh, safe water pours from the tap. I am healthy enough to work a small garden that keeps me in touch with small gardeners all around the world, many of whom depend on their plots for all their food, and reminds me that the natural world was made to be favourably disposed toward human beings, so perhaps I should be more careful with and protective of the natural world. I pack groceries at a food pantry with people who could be doing something else with their time, but who took it to heart when they heard Jesus' parable ask, 'When did we see you hungry?' And occasionally I have an invitation which gives me hope, an assignment like speaking to a bunch of university students who were wise enough to know a novena for peace was powerful and positive action in a broken world.

'Now hope that is seen is not hope' (8:24). But it is an invitation to grow in faith and trust, to learn that our struggle to hope in the face of so much hopelessness is a gift *to* God and to each other. While I seldom wait patiently, I might be able to wait *faithfully*, along with all the faithful and all of creation, along with Jesus who died on the cross, and was buried in a tomb, and—amazingly—was raised on the third day, which nobody, least of all his closest associates, expected.

Finally hope itself does not depend on us, but is gift. The Christian's hope originates in the nature of God and what God has already done in Jesus Christ. (Recall 8:1–11.) Hope's trajectory is toward God's future, but it is not a matter of 'pie in the sky by and by.' J. M. Everts reminds us that a Christian's hope anticipates the future and brings it into the present. 'Hope is not defined by present realities but by God's purposes for the future.' 'Hope is an encouragement to believers in the midst of suffering, but it also prevents believers from being content with present circumstances.' Hope 'leads reality toward the promised transformation' (DPL 416 & 417). However veiled, that transformation is in process now and occasionally visible to those with eyes to see, those who are looking for it, living toward it, assisting its coming. As blind Bartimaeus requested of Jesus, 'Master, let me receive my sight' (Mark 8:51).

For Prayer and Pondering

1. Because he was a good pastor to early Christian congregations and knew the sufferings of many of them, Paul often spoke about hope and perseverance. Texts that relate to and illuminate Romans 8:24–25 (in its context) include 1 Corinthians 2:9–10, 2 Corinthians 5:6–7, and the prayer that opens Colossians, 1:3–8, another church to which he writes which he has not visited. You might find those texts valuable as you think about hope in suffering.

2. What are the 'strategies' that keep your hope alive in situations of apparent hopelessness? What do you do while waiting for hope which cannot be seen?

ROMANS 8:26–30

Help

26 Likewise the Spirit helps us in our weakness; for we do not know how to pray as we ought, but that very Spirit intercedes with sighs too deep for words. **27** And God, who searches the heart, knows what is the mind of the Spirit, because the Spirit intercedes for the saints according to the will of God. **28** We know that all things work together for good for those who love God, who are called according to his purpose. **29** For those whom he foreknew he also predestined to be conformed to the image of his Son, in order that he might be the firstborn within a large family. **30** And those whom he predestined he also called; and those whom he called he also justified; and those whom he justified he also glorified.

Points of Interest

Apparently Paul understands that 'unseen hope' can seem cold comfort in actual, individual situations of suffering, so he reminds the Roman Christians that the Spirit helps them in weakness (8:26), that God will bring good for those who love God (8:28), and, best of all, that 'God is for us' (8:31). The second half of Romans 8 is devoted to encouraging the Roman Christians. Verses 26–30 begin with the adverb 'likewise', *hosautos*, a strong link to what has preceded, as is the repetition of a form of the word 'groaning' (not apparent in the English translation 'sighs too deep for words') which appeared in v. 22 and reappears in v. 26.

Verses 28 and 29 are full of interesting questions for New Testament scholars and for theologians. Here they are largely outside the scope of our exploration. Very briefly, there is a text-critical problem which leads to at least four ways of translating 8:28.[50] The commentaries remind us that the thrust of the verse is that what happens to 'those who love God' is part of God's plan for their good. (How this can be, I have found, is often not always clear.) To believe it is part of the hope suggested in the previous two verses.

Similarly, verse 29 has been a source of controversy in theological, and subsequently church, history due largely to the words 'foreknew' and 'predestined'. 'Foreknew' (from *proorao*) includes God's 'all knowing' nature and the fact that linear time as we know and live it, does not apply to God for whom time is always present tense. That God 'sees beforehand' does not necessarily mean that God causes. God may *know* something will happen without *causing* it to happen. Knox puts it this way: 'Although many things happen which are not *in accordance* with God's will, nothing occurs *outside* his will—that is, outside the area where he works and rules and not only in judgment, but also with healing and creative power' (Knox 115).

This influences how we interpret 'predestined' (*proorizo*) which is more problematic as it means something like 'decide from the beginning' (*pro*–before; *orizo*–decide, determine, designate). It is probably important to remember that Paul is speaking in a corporate sense and without the benefit (or burden?) of 2,000 years of Christian interpretation. Augustine interpreted the text in an individual sense, which has led to various confusions.

The point in Romans 8:28–30 is that those called according to God's purpose are 'to be conformed to the image (*ikon*) of his

---

[50] On these verses see Joseph A. Fitzmyer, SJ, *Romans* (Anchor Bible Commentary; New York: Doubleday, 1993).

Son' (v. 29). This is a significant movement from what was said in 8:12–17. Now believers are not just adopted children and heirs—as wonderful as that is—but the image or likeness of Christ himself. The trajectory in Romans is from slaves, to children and heirs, to the bearers of Christ's likeness. Paul wrote similarly to the church at Corinth: 'And all of us, with unveiled faces, seeing the glory of the Lord as though reflected in a mirror, *are being transformed into the same image*, from one degree of glory to another; for this comes from the Lord, the Spirit' (2 Cor. 3:18, italics mine. Rom. 8:28–30 and 2 Cor. 3:17–18 serve as mutual glosses. And see Phil. 3:21).

What God has known and planned ahead of time for believers is that we shall *become* what we see in Jesus Christ. This is the general consensus of both Roman Catholic and Protestant scholarship. Fitzmyer says that God's plan is that those God calls are to reproduce in themselves the image of Christ.[51] C. K. Barrett notes that when God's purpose is realized, believers shall share God's likeness.[52] C. H. Dodd concurs, noting that 'whatever else salvation is, it will be sharing the likeness of Christ.'[53]

Reflection

At this point Romans 8 becomes a great hymn to hope. It tells us that, in Jesus, God has done for us what we could not do for ourselves, that God has chosen both to dwell *in* us (via the Spirit), and to adopt us as children and heirs. That summarizes 8:1–17, in light of which Paul rather audaciously says in 8:18–25

---

[51] Fitzmyer, *Romans*, 525.

[52] C. K. Barrett, *Epistle to the Romans* (London: Adam & Charles Black, 1957/84), 170.

[53] C. H. Dodd, *The Epistle of Paul to the Romans* (London: Collins/Fontana, 1932/59), 156.

that our personal sufferings are not all that important; our assignment is to hope, and we will have divine, spiritual help to do so. 'I consider that the sufferings of this present time,' writes the guy who has been beaten and imprisoned and shipwrecked and all the rest of it, 'are not worth comparing with the glory about to be revealed to us' (8:18). Indeed, in light of the suffering of the whole cosmos, my suffering, important though it might be to me and for my spiritual transformation, is hardly worth the proverbial hill of beans. It is a startling way of reminding me that I am not the centre of the universe/cosmos. Incidentally, neither are you.

It is not about me or any one of us. It is about God. We are not the subject; God is. We are the objects and, oddly enough, this grammatical fact is the ground of Christian hope because the power behind the universe, its subject, if you will, is not against us, or even neutral, but benevolent, for us, comes to be with us, to indwell, empower, and comfort us. God provides us, all of us, with spiritual help. I need it. Most of the time, big time! I resonate when Paul says, 'I do not understand my own actions. For I do not do what I want, but I do the very thing I hate' (7:15). 'I can will what is right, but I cannot do it. For I do not do the good I want, but the evil I do not want is what I do' (7:18-19). Any chance you share my predicament?

What Paul was talking about was much deeper than the common moralization about it. This is not about, 'I know I should not eat crisps or ice cream, or Cadbury bars—you fill in the blanks—but I buy and eat a large packet anyhow.' We could substitute any of the Seven Deadly Sins—lust or anger or avarice, you choose your favourite—for crisps. We know what we should not do, but we do it. We cannot help ourselves. And that is because, as Paul has explained in chapters 5-7, sin is not always volitional. Sin is a power that influences us, and all the human will power (or 'won't power', as in I *won't* eat any more crisps!) in the world cannot stand up to it alone.

This is bad enough, but the deeper problem, the one Paul addresses in 8: 26–30, is that we do not know how to access the means of help and deliverance. We do not know how to pray as we ought. Not only are we morally impotent, we are spiritually clueless. We do not know how to pray, what to say, what to ask for, how to intercede, or even if it is *verbal* prayer that is called for. The older I get, the truer this is. The situations for which I might intercede are so complex, so multi-faceted, so morally ambiguous, that I do not know how to address God about them. I do not *know* what should be done, and I often suspect that what I pray for might be what *I* want or *I* think and not God's will.

Actually, this might be a good thing, this deep, wordless yearning for God's intervention in human complexity. In addition to the fact that it might save me from asking God for rubbishy, small-minded solutions (mine!), it might teach me that the deepest, most authentic prayer might have nothing to do with words, a very hard thought for a writer. If verses 26–27 suggest anything, it is, in the words of C. H. Dodd, that inarticulate aspiration may be the deepest form of prayer, the work of the Spirit within us.[54] It might teach us with existential truthfulness that prayer itself is God's work within us. Indeed, Fitzmyer asserts, 'Paul recognizes the "ineffable sight" of the Spirit as the source of all genuine Christian prayers.'[55]

Just as, left to our own devices, we cannot save ourselves, or do the good we want to do, or avoid the evil we know as evil, we cannot pray, *really* pray, on our own. Prayer, itself, is the

---

[54] Dodd 150.
[55] Fitzmyer, *Spiritual Exercises*, 141.

work of God in us, another of God's gifts *to* us. Paul explains that 'the Spirit helps us in our weakness,' and 'the Spirit intercedes for the saints according to the will of God' (8:26-7).

The Greek word for 'intercede' is *proseuchomai,* a compound verb made up of *pros,* toward or for the sake of, and *euchomai,* to pray, to wish, to long for. It is the most commonly used word for 'prayer' in the New Testament and includes *both* verbal prayer and inarticulate longing.[56] 'Intercede' is a Latinate word; it means 'to go from,' in this case to go from one to another, from God to us to God. Earlier in the chapter Paul wrote, 'the Spirit of God dwells in you' (8:9). That indwelling presence is the connection between us and God, and this is exactly what Jesus promised about the Spirit, the Paraclete, the Comforter in chapters 14–16 of John's Gospel.

And it gets better. The Holy Spirit connects us to God in the deepest parts of ourselves, the parts deeper than language, the parts we do not even know about ourselves, and the risen Christ lives eternally to do just this. Paul speaks of 'Christ Jesus, who died, … who was raised, who is at the right hand of God, who indeed intercedes for us' (8:34). This is also what the writer of Hebrews understood about Christ's eternal mission: 'he is able for all time to save those who approach God through him, since he always lives to make intercession for them' (Heb. 7:25). Jesus Christ lives to make the connection between us and God. What greater spiritual help could there be?

This is why Paul can make the outrageous claim 'all things work together for good for those who love God, who are called according to his purpose' (8:28). This affirmation of Christian

---

[56] For more see Bonnie Thurston 'Prayer in the New Testament,' in Mark Kiley et al, (eds), *Prayer from Alexander to Constantine: A Critical Anthology* (London & New York: Routledge, 1997), 207–210.

destiny is the basis for the hope in 8:17–27.[57] Note, however, Paul does *not* say that everything works out fine for everybody, but that everything works toward good (it is a process, not an end result; an efficient, not a final cause) for those who love God and are called by God. Behind everything is God's loving call, whether or not we listen for it or can hear it clearly. God is resident in everything and every situation, calling to us if we but had 'ears to hear'.

Greek philosophers like Seneca (*On Providence*) and Epictetus (*Discourse* 1:16) wrote in defence of God's providence. What Paul knew that they did not know was Jesus Christ, the proof incarnate of God's providence, 'in whom every one of God's promises is a "Yes"' (2 Cor. 1:20). Jesus came to be *with* the created universe and, when He departed, sent the Holy Spirit as the conduit of the spiritual help that, at the right hand of God, He eternally dispenses. '[T]hose whom he predestined he also called; and those whom he called he also justified; and those whom he justified he also glorified' (8:30). The aorist tense of the verb suggests believers already have in part their ultimate glorification. (See also 1 Cor. 6:11.) The plan is that those God calls, and for whom the Spirit intercedes, are to reproduce in themselves the image of Christ. No wonder suffering is involved: it is hard to clean out all that mouldy, internal junk to make room for Jesus and the Holy Spirit! But the great promise is that those bearing the image of dust *will* bear, 'show forth' and 'carry' the image of heaven (1 Cor. 15:49). 'All of us,' Paul wrote to the Corinthians, 'are being trans-formed into the same image from one degree of glory to another ...' (2 Cor. 3:18). Astonishing.

---

[57] Fitzmyer, *Romans*, 521.

Right. So where does this leave us in the midst of the muddle that is our lives? With the promise of spiritual help, with Paul's conviction that, in the very core of our being (the heart, 8:27), the aspect of divinity we call the Holy Spirit is clearing the pathway between us and God, who promises that, no matter how rotten things are—and they *can* be very rotten indeed—in God's mysterious way they are working toward a heavenly purpose: the full realization of the Christ image in everyone and everything. It is as Fitzmyer asserts, 'With both God and Christ on our side, our eternal destiny is assured.'[58]

For Prayer and Pondering

1. Think and pray a bit about the astonishing idea that *you* are intended to be an ikon of Christ, an image of Him that makes Him present wherever you are.

2. What, exactly, is 'wordless prayer?' If you know something of contemplative prayer or the writings of Thomas Merton OCSO or Thomas Keating OCSO or John Main OSB or Lawrence Freeman OSB, or of their common source *The Cloud of Unknowing*, how might you introduce it in the parish and from the pulpit?

---

[58] Fitzmyer, *Spiritual Exercises*, 152.

ROMANS 8:31–39

Promises

31 What then are we to say about these things? If God
is for us, who is against us? 32 He who did not
withhold his own Son, but gave him up for all of us,
will he not with him also give us everything else? 33
Who will bring any charge against God's elect? It is
God who justifies. 34 Who is to condemn? It is Christ
Jesus, who died, yes, who was raised, who is at the
right hand of God, who indeed intercedes for us. 35
Who will separate us from the love of Christ? Will
hardship, or distress, or persecution, or famine, or
nakedness, or peril, or sword? 36 As it is written, 'For
your sake we are being killed all day long; we are
accounted as sheep to be slaughtered.' 37 No, in all
these things we are more than conquerors through him
who loved us. 38 For I am convinced that neither
death, nor life, nor angels, nor rulers, nor things
present, nor things to come, nor powers, 39 nor height,
nor depth, nor anything else in all creation, will be
able to separate us from the love of God in Christ
Jesus our Lord.

Points of Interest

Joseph Fitzmyer rightfully calls 8:31–39 'a hymn to the love of
God for human beings manifested through Jesus Christ. ... Paul
concludes this second doctrinal section of the epistle with a
rhetorical, even hymnic, passage about the love of God
manifest in what Christ Jesus has done for humanity.'[59] Several
scholars suggest it has two sections: vv. 31–37, which raise

___

[59] Fitzmyer *Spiritual Exercises*, 150–151.

seven rhetorical questions, and vv. 38–39, a strong statement of Christian assurance which has, in effect, been the subject of Romans 5–8. Wright asserts that 'The argument of this paragraph is ... the same as that of 5:6–10' (NIB 10:609; cf. 1 Cor. 15:20–28).

Romans 8:31–39 is replete with allusions to Hebrew scripture. Those allusions affect the meaning of the passage and suggest that many of the letter's first recipients were expected to understand their implications. Verse 31 echoes Psalm 118:6: 'With the Lord on my side I do not fear./What can mortals do to me?' Verse 32 recalls the story of Abraham's willingness to sacrifice Isaac (Gen. 22:1–19). Isaiah 50:4–9 may stand behind vv. 33–34, and v. 34 may also allude to Isaiah 53:12. The phrase 'at the right hand of God' in v. 34 recalls Psalm 110:1, a verse often quoted in early Christianity with Christological implications. Verse 36 quotes Psalm 44:22, and may allude to Isaiah 53:7.

The passage is a tour de force of Paul's use of scriptural allusion. It also includes the familiar court-of-law trope from Hebrew scripture and uses legal language that the first recipients of the letter would have recognized. This 'law court setting' was familiar to Paul and other Jewish Christians from many passages in Hebrew scripture which are framed as 'trials' (e.g. Job 1-2, Is. 41:1–42:4, Ps. 50, 82). N. T. Wright makes a convincing case that the covenantal meaning of 'righteousness', the subject of the Romans letter, was 'shaped by the Second Temple Jewish setting of the law court,' and 'was the status of the successful party when the case had been decided' and 'also denoted the appropriate activity of the judge.' Since Paul thought the covenant was made so the Creator could rescue the whole creation (recall 8:18–25), justice was 'setting to rights that which is out of joint, restoring things as they should be' (NIB

62

10:398, 399). '… God's righteousness, seen in terms of covenant faithfulness and through the image of the law court, was to be the instrument of putting the world to rights—of what we might call cosmic restorative justice' (NIB 10:400).

Several Jewish writings frame the relationship between Gentile nations and Israel in terms of a cosmic lawsuit. (For examples see Ps. 143, Dan. 7, and 4 Ezra.) Rome 'prided itself on being … the capital of justice, the source from which justice would flow throughout the world' (NIB 10:404). A temple to the Roman goddess Iustitia had been established in AD 13. Imperial Rome and the virtue Iustitia were so closely aligned that she was sometimes called 'Augusta.' To assert that the Gospel of Jesus Christ was the fulfilment of God's justice/ righteousness presented another source of conflict with Empire.

Whatever else it is, Romans 8:31–39 summarizes not only Paul's message in chapter 8, but chapters 5 to 8, and perhaps the whole first part of the letter, and, since the time of Paul has been a source of immeasurable comfort to Christians.

Reflection

Romans 8 is a chapter full of extraordinary promises. Some of the more astonishing ones are as follows:

~ There is … now no condemnation for those who are in Christ Jesus (v. 1).

~ If the Spirit of him who raised Jesus from the dead dwells in you, he who raised Christ from the dead will give life to your mortal bodies (v. 11).

~ … all who are led by the Spirit of God are children of God (v. 14).

~ … if children, then heirs, heirs of God and joint heirs with Christ … (v. 17).

~ ... the Spirit helps us in our weakness ... (v. 26).

~ ... the Spirit intercedes with sighs too deep for words (v. 26).

~ ... all things work together for good for those who love God, who are called according to his purpose (v. 28).

It is in light of all these promises that Paul asks rhetorically in v. 31 'What then are we to say about these things?' (I think we might start with 'thank you!') The question is in the style of Stoic diatribe that characterizes this letter (see 'Textual and Stylistic Considerations', p. 12–14), and the rhetoric is forensic. The setting is now, by allusion, that of the law court. There is a trial in progress. In chapters 1–4 of Romans Paul has spoken of the 'crimes' of which all humanity is guilty. Romans 5–8 describe what God has set out to do to address that problem. Romans 8 summarizes the first half of the letter. It is Paul's 'closing argument' in the case.

Paul's argument proceeds like this: God gave the only Son God had on our behalf to cancel out our crimes. The magnitude of this gift proves that there is nothing that God will not give. Since God in Jesus has *already* declared us 'not guilty', nobody can bring charges against us or condemn us. You cannot charge the already acquitted. The basis of our confidence in our 'not guilty' verdict is the character of God, shown in Christ. As C. H. Dodd so beautifully wrote, 'The Judge becomes our Advocate.'[60] The one who has authority to pass sentence on us has become our defence attorney.

Two millennia of Christian theology later, it is easy to take this amazing transference for granted. We think we know all about the atonement. Jesus died for our sins. (Blah, blah, blah.) But imagine if you will, how this sounded in the ears of those

---

[60] Dodd 159.

first-century Roman Christians, Christians for whom the Neronian persecutions were heating up. *De facto* to be a Christian in Rome was to be a petty criminal. Or not so petty if one publically claims Jesus and not Caesar is Lord. That is sedition. As previously noted, Christianity was *religio illicita*, an illegal religion (which it remained until the fourth century) in a world where religion and the state were often inseparable. A Christian might very well be on trial if he or she were so lucky as to have recourse to the criminal justice system by virtue of being a Roman citizen. The majority were not.

It is against this background that we must read the legal language of verses 31–34, and against the threat of the arena and the wild beasts that we must read verses 34 and the following. 'Who will separate us from the love of Christ? Will hardship (*thliphis*, 'pressure'), or distress (*stenochoria*, 'anguish'), or persecution, or famine, or nakedness, or peril, or sword?' I imagine that sounded rather different in the ears of one rotting away in a Roman prison (where the *only* things provided were the cell and the chains) waiting to be thrown to the lions or hacked to death by gladiators for the entertainment of the *hoi polloi*.

The quotation in v. 36 from Psalm 44:22 (and containing other allusions, see 'Points of Interest' for this section) about being killed, being 'sheep to be slaughtered', is taken from a psalm that is a community lament about the injustices done to Israel. At least some of the recipients of Paul's Roman letter would have understood it as shorthand for 'God's people have always suffered. If you think election or chosen-ness is a cosmic "get out of jail free card", you are dead (!) wrong.' And what Christians reading that verse would have missed in it Jesus' own story in miniature? And pondered their own immediate future?

But the amazing promise is that, even in the face of profound suffering, God's heirs are '*more* than conquerors' (v. 37, italics mine). What an assertion. The great Roman military machine was conqueror, not persecuted minorities. And the promise is not just that the persecuted will be delivered, which would be very good news indeed, it is that the persecuted will *become more than* conquerors. How did that sound to Roman Christians as they lived under the most formidable army and political system then extant? What would it mean to conquer the mighty Romans? The function of the conquered is always to show the strength of the conquerors. For the Christians to conquer the Romans was to demonstrate the power of Christ. (It would *not* mean that the new conquerors would be given licence to mistreat the newly conquered, to do unto them as they had been done unto.)

But the promise is even more astonishing than that the guilty are exonerated by the very judge who might rightfully convict and that the persecuted are conquerors. The promise extends beyond this world to the cosmic powers and to time personified. (Recall our discussion of Rom. 8:18–23.) The last two verses, vv. 38 and 39, with their catalogue of contrasting pairs, speak not only of the powers of this world, but of the spiritual world. The *real* enemy of human life in Roman times was not Rome itself, but the astrological powers that people believed determined human destiny, what Paul in several letters calls 'the powers' or 'the elemental spirits of the universe'. (See, for example, Col. 2:8–23, Eph. 6:12.) They have been rendered impotent (cf. Phil. 2:10–11 and Col. 1:15–20). Not even time itself, 'things present, nor things to come', separates the Christian from the God who, at creation, *made* time: evening and morning, a day, a stretch of time.

Nothing is able to separate God's people from God's love. Note that the text does not say 'from God,' but from God's *love* in (the Greek *hen* here might be read instrumentally, 'by means of') Christ Jesus. Sometimes the faithful do feel separated from God. Setting aside the fact that how we *feel* in the spiritual life is not of critical importance, this sense of separation from God is the very worst thing that can happen to a deeply faithful person. That experience was for Jesus the root of the horror in the Garden of Gethsemane and is heard in His cry of dereliction from the Cross in Mark's Gospel: 'My God, my God, why have you forsaken me?' (Mark 15: 34).

While the reality is that a human being (even the perfect human being) may *feel* separated from God, he or she is never, under any circumstances, separated from God's love. An important point. For just as 'all things work together for good for those who love God, who are called according to his purpose' (8:28), God is always extending the Divine Self in love toward creation. That we cannot always perceive it does not negate the reality of God's self-giving.

Romans 8, which affirms so clearly that the love of God poured out in Jesus Christ is the basis of Christian hope, closes with a great hymn to hope. It acknowledges that human life is uncertain, dreadfully uncertain. We human beings *are* subject to hardship, distress, persecution, famine, nakedness, peril, sword, eccentric behaviour in positions of leadership, and insanity in the halls of power. We always have been, that is the human reality. But the assertion of the Apostle Paul, so eloquently expressed here, is that human suffering, inevitable or inflicted, does not have the last word. God's love, which is fixed and certain, does.

Paul's assurance is not that of rational argument, but of personal conviction. It certainly has the ringing, authentic quality of deep personal confidence. Paul is persuaded, both by the witness and interpretation of Jewish scripture and by his own experience, that God's promises are true because the promiser, the great cosmic lover, is trustworthy. Christians are not those 'who have no hope' (1 Thess. 4:13); we stand on the bedrock of trustworthy promises because the promiser is trustworthy. We may be required to 'hope for what we do not see' and 'wait for it with patience' (8:25); but in the final analysis God does not 'give us up' (8:24, 26, 28). 'God is for us', (8:31) and nothing in all creation 'will separate us from the love of Christ' (8:35). God has not abandoned what God created. N. T. Wright reminds us that 'Paul speaks of God's love as the ultimate security.' 'The love of God ... proposes a hermeneutic of trust ... a knowing that is born of being loved and of loving in return' (NIB 10: 617 and 618). The justice of God as punitive or juridical is not the final word. Love is. In Paul's time and in our own, this fact is the best news going.

For Prayer and Pondering

1. If you have had the experience, revisit a time when you *felt* God's absence.

What circumstances surrounded that perception? What gave you hope in it, or at least allowed you to persevere in and through it? How does it look to you now in retrospect? What did you learn?

2. In light of whatever is the 'horror of the day', how does one assert, much less preach, the assurance of God's love declared by Paul? (You cannot take people where you have not been, preachers, and they will know if you preach what you do not believe.)

A Concluding Note

In his essay, 'Preaching Romans Today,' Thomas Long suggests that 'Romans is about how life looks when people have bet everything on the righteousness of God, confident that they will not be put to shame.'[61] Romans 8 is not only a summary of the letter to this point, and the hinge that links that material with what follows, it is the Pauline Gospel in miniature, and, as it did in first-century Rome, continues to sound a note of encouragement and hope to Christians whatever their circumstances. It is this very confidence, encouragement, and hope in what God was doing in the death and resurrection of Jesus, and continues to do in us through the Holy Spirit, that is the Christian's security and Christianity's best offering to an insecure and unstable world. And all of this is God's doing and from God's love.

In *Meeting God in Paul*, Rowan Williams explains, 'the new world does not come into being because we are brilliant, holy, loving and reconciling, because we are not. But God is; and anything that happens to bring this newness into the world is God's work, from first to last.' And furthermore, '… God's future is alive here and now, and it is us. We … are living *on the other side of the end of the world*, living God's life—to which the whole life of the universe is being drawn … by a timeless and unchanging love seeking to reconcile or heal what is broken in the created world at every level'[62] (italics in original). 'God's future is alive … and it is us' beautifully summarizes the message of Romans 8. It is a glorious and sobering reality and, like the chapter itself, gives us a great deal to ponder, pray, and preach.

---

[61] Long 273.
[62] Williams 53 and 69.